Distinguished Service

University of Wisconsin Faculty and Staff
Helping to Build Organizations in the State

....

A COLLECTION OF CASE HISTORIES
ON ORGANIZATION BUILDING
IN CELEBRATION OF
WISCONSIN'S SESQUICENTENNIAL

Ayse Somersan

Emeritus Professor and Dean
UW-Madison/UW-Extension

NEW PAST PRESS, INC.
Friendship, Wisconsin

Distinguished Service

University of Wisconsin Faculty and Staff Helping to Build Organizations in the State

Ayse Somersan
Emeritus Professor and Dean, UW-Madison/Extension

New Past Press, Inc.
Friendship, Wisconsin
General Editor: Michael J. Goc
Publishing Assistants: Erika Hall and Christy Ciecko
Cover and Page Design: Jay Jocham

Library of Congress Cataloging in Publication Data

Somersan, Ayse.
    Distinguished service : University of Wisconsin faculty and staff helping to build organizations in the state : a collection of case histories on organization building in celebration of Wisconsin's sesquicentennial / Ayse Somersan.
        p. cm. Includes bibliographical references (p.) and index.
    ISBN 0-938627-38-4 (alk. paper)
    1. University of Wisconsin. University Extension – History. 2. University of Wisconsin. University Extension – Faculty – Biography. I. Title.
    LC6252.W6S65 1997
378.1'75'09775–dc21
                                                         97-31906
                                                                CIP

CONTENTS

Acknowledgements

Advisory Committee

Gerald Campbell, Professor, UW-Madison/Extension

Ellen Fitzsimmons, Professor/Administrator, UW-Extension

Shirley Johnson, Emeritus Professor/Librarian, UW-Extension

Leonard Maurer, Senior Lecturer/Administrator, College of Agricultural and Life Sciences, UW-Madison

Donald Peterson, Emeritus Professor/Administrator, College of Agricultural and Life Sciences, UW-Madison/Extension

Special Advisors

Patrick G. Boyle, UW Regent, Emeritus Professor, UW-Madison and Chancellor, UW-Extension

Theodore Shannon, Emeritus Professor, UW-Madison and Dean, UW-Extension

Luke Lamb, Emeritus Professor/Director, UW-Extension

Photography

Del Brown, Photographer

Wolfgang Hoffman, Photographer, Department of Agricultural Journalism CALS, UW-Madison

Bernard Schermetzler, Archivist, Memorial Library, UW-Madison

Steven Sundell, Librarian, Music Library, UW-Madison

Cathy Prescher and William Herrick
News Services and Publications, UW-Milwaukee

Editing

Sheila Mulcahy, Distinguished Institutional Planner
UW-Extension

Personal Interviews And/Or Historical Information Support

The Arts

Harv Thompson, Chair, Department of Liberal Studies and the Arts
UW-Madison/Extension

David Peterson, Emeritus Professor, Arts, UW-Madison/Extension

Richard Wolf, Emeritus Professor, Arts, UW-Madison/Extension

Jerold Apps, Emer. Prof., Cont.& Voc. Ed., UW-Madison/Extension

Robert Graves, Graves Associates, Spring Green

Patricia Blankenburg, Wisconsin Manufacturers and Commerce and Wisconsin Sesquicentennial Commission

Cedric Vig, Emeritus Superintendent, Rhinelander School District

Dean Amhaus, Wisconsin Sesquicentennial Commission

Elayne Clipper-Nelson, President, Wisconsin Regional Writers Association

Jeffrey Bartell, President, Wisconsin Foundation for the Arts

Fannie Taylor, Emeritus Professor, Arts, UW-Madison

George Tzougros, Executive Director, Wisconsin Arts Board

Cooperatives

Truman Graf, Emeritus Professor, UW-Madison/Extension

Frank Groves, Emeritus Professor, UW-Madison/Extension

Richard Vilstrup, Emeritus Professor, UW-Madison/Extension

Peter Giacomini, CEO, AgSource Cooperative Services

Rod Nilsestuen, President and CEO, Wisconsin Federation of Cooperatives

Joan Behr, Vice-President-Communication, Foremost Farms-USA

Forage Councils

Dwayne Rohweder, Emeritus Professor, Agronomy, UW-Madison/Extension

Dan Undersander, Professor of Agronomy, UW-Madison/Extension

Forestry

Ron Giese, Chair, Department of Forestry, UW-Madison

Gordon Cunnigham, Emeritus Professor, Forestry
UW-Madison/Extension

Chris Hauge, Emeritus Professor
College of Natural Resources, UW-Stevens Point/Extension

Theodore Peterson, Emeritus Professor, Forestry
UW-Madison/Extension

Thomas Rausch, Retired Forester/Administrator
Wisconsin Department of Natural Resources

Health And Human Issues

Roger Williams, Chair, Department of Professional Development and
Applied Studies, UW-Madison/Extension

Harriet Shetler, Founder, Dane Co. Alliance of Mental Health

Urban Neighborhoods

Reuben Harpole, Senior Outreach Specialist, Center for Urban Community
Development, UW-Milwaukee/Extension

Belden Paulson, Emeritus Professor, former chair, Center for Urban
Community Development, UW-Milwaukee/Extension

Agnes Cobbs, Retired Outreach Specialist, Center for Urban Community Development, UW-Milwaukee/Extension

Lakes Partnership

Lowell Klessig, Professor, College of Natural Resources, UW-Stevens Point/Extension

Robert Korth, Outreach Specialist, Extension Lakes Program College of Natural Resources, UW-Stevens Point/Extension

Wisconsin Farm Progress Days

Henry Ahlgren, Emeritus Professor and Chancellor, UW-Madison/Extension

Al Francour, Emeritus Professor/Administrator, UW-Extension

Donald Peterson, Emeritus Professor/Administrator, UW-Madison/Extension

Art Peterson, Emeritus Professor, Soils, UW-Madison/Extension

Tourism

Donald Schink, Emeritus Professor, UW-Extension

Herman Smith, Emeritus Professor, UW-Extension

Thomas Coenen, Lobbyist, Wisconsin Tourism Federation

Sue Sadowske, Emeritus Professor, UW-Extension

Eugene Radloff, Emeritus Professor, UW-Extension

Women's Movement

Constance Threinen, Emeritus Sr. Outreach Spec., Women's Education Resources & Division of Outreach, UW-Madison/Extension

Marian Thompson, Emeritus Professor, Women's Education Resources & Division of Outreach, UW-Madison/Extension

Rural Leadership

Alan Anderson, Professor, UW-Extension

Mary Maier, Program Assis. & Manager, Wisconsin Rural Leadership Program, UW-Extension & WRLP, Inc.

Kickapoo Reserve

Alan Anderson, Professor, UW-Extension

Marcy West, Executive Director, Kickapoo Reserve Management Board

Learning Institute

Katie Burnham, Executive Director
The Learning Institute for Nonprofit Organizations Madison

Terry Gibson, Professor/Administrator, UW-Madison/Extension

AUTHOR'S NOTE

The idea for this book came from Dr. Donald Hanna, former Chancellor of UW-Extension. It was among a long list of projects UW-Extension would undertake in celebration of Wisconsin's sesquicentennial. We both felt that organization building activities of UW faculty and staff were not sufficiently highlighted in previous publications on the Wisconsin Idea or in published institutional histories.

This has turned out to be an immensely satisfying project for me. I have discovered significant contributions of faculty and staff that even I didn't know, despite having been a part of UW-Extension for over two decades. The contributions of UW-Extension and its campus partners to the quality of life and the economy of Wisconsin are varied and multi-dimensional. This book's focus is only one of those dimensions--organization building. Even with this narrow focus, many more books need to be written on the topic of organization building to do justice to all campus and departmental contributions, as well to the local organizations that county Extension faculty and staff have helped build and nurture over the last fifty years.

The research and the writing had to be completed in eight months, in order to get the publication ready for the start of the sesquicentennial celebration. Thus, the coverage could only be illustrative, not exhaustive. My Advisory Committee helped identify topic areas, but the choices were mine. I know I have omitted important work that I hope gets highlighted in future books.

I am grateful for the help and support of individuals who have shared with me their memories. I have been privileged to have access to their files and photo albums, and to be welcomed into their homes. Each section was reviewed by the principals and I have incorporated their comments and suggestions into the documents. I have identified the people who generously contributed and the documents I have used in different parts of this book. Words don't do justice to my feelings of gratitude. The errors and omissions, however, are still mine.

I have great respect for the talent, creativity and commitment of the faculty and staff and their external partners who are the organization builders identified in this book. I hope I have done justice to their vast contributions.

—Ayse Somersan
Emeritus Professor and Dean
UW-Madison/Extension
June, 1997

INTRODUCTION

$\mathcal{T}$he history of **The Wisconsin Idea** has been researched and ably documented by historians of higher education and others. This concept, which has distinguished Wisconsin from other places, has a rich and multi-faceted history which shows the state and the university maturing together over 150 years.

The outreach activities of University of Wisconsin faculty pre-date the establishment of the Extension Division in 1906. Early continuing education work includes teachers and farmers institutes, experimental farms demonstrating farming practices and research results, bulletins that would revolutionize the dairy industry, policy development work that would change the social fabric of Wisconsin and the nation, lectures delivered in far corners of the state to inform and enrich the citizenry, and institution-building, which would support electrification, soil conservation, youth and family development. One can hardly identify a facet of Wisconsin's history where the University of Wisconsin has not been an integral part of change and growth.

This book builds on that rich tradition. The focus is a dimension of outreach and extension work which is often overlooked in historical accounts of faculty contributions beyond research and classroom teaching. It is the area of organizational development and institution building — University faculty helping people of similar interests and avocations form associations and organizations to learn from each other, further a cause, shape public policy and provide an organized way for University staff to deliver education.

Organization building is often a part of other major dimensions of outreach and extension work by UW faculty and staff. I would identify these dimensions as formal and informal continuing education for professionals, business and industry, workers and the general public; applied research; informational and cultural programming through public radio and television; leadership development and the building of human capacity. They cover all disciplines and socio-economic and political fronts. Most of the activity is organized through UW-Extension and its collaborative relationship with the other UW universities and centers and with the Wisconsin counties and state agencies. But there is still a great deal of service to the state, beyond the organized educational activities through UW-Extension, which is individual and at the initiative of faculty as the opportunity presents itself.

The focus of this book is the post-war era of roughly the last fifty years, 1940's to the present. The stories cover statewide, regional and national organizations. Thus, the "organization builders" are faculty and staff in campus departments across the University of Wisconsin. There is a vast amount of community and county level organization building by county Extension faculty and staff which is not covered in this book. To do justice to those efforts requires county level histories or, possibly, single theme focus.

The main players in this book are the faculty and staff whose commitment and creativity resulted in a vast array of innovative educational programs. But they didn't act alone. They were joined by thousands of volunteers, cooperating agencies, organizations and businesses, both public and private, on the local, state and national levels. I have tried to highlight the contributions of public and private partners, the all-important collaborators and leaders, in each story. I know I've missed many.

Finally, the stories of UW faculty and staff included in this book are illustrative, not exhaustive, of organization building activity across different fronts. All the individuals have a connection to UW-Extension, not only because of the funding and institutional realities of the time period, but also because historical reports and accounts of organization-building work have been preserved through the culture of accountability of this UW institution.

PROFILE OF THE ORGANIZATION BUILDERS

There are striking commonalities in the organization builders included in this book. The common threads are so strong that a profile emerges as one goes across the many themes. The following characteristics constitute the profile of the organization builder:

- Accomplished in disciplinary area.
- Visionary, creative and committed.
- Exceptional communication skills.
- Strong personal bonds with public and private leaders in the field.
- Public spirited and service oriented.
- Able to secure administrative support and funding.
- Able to give and share credit.
- High energy and mobility.

Additionally, these organization builders were most willing to do the grunt work that is so essential to organizing and creating associations and institutions. These include such activities as meeting arrangements, mailings, chairing and directing, minutes, by-laws, newsletter development and a multitude of other details without which there would be no lasting organization in place.

Thinking great thoughts is only part of the organization building formula. Using the resources of your office, being willing to do what's necessary, nurturing the leaders who will carry on, are critical elements of organization building. It is only when all the pieces are in place that one can "graduate" the new organization. If you do it well, they won't even remember you were there!

CASE SELECTION AND INFORMATION COLLECTION

The identification of cases to be considered for inclusion in this book relied on advisory committee input, interviews with retired administrators, leads obtained from published historical material, suggestions from retired faculty and staff, and personal knowledge. The Advisory Committee members were very helpful in defining the broad areas of educational activity — arts, natural resources, agriculture, etc. Interviews with retired administrators provided the next level of detail in terms of their personal knowledge or their identification of sources who would know of organization building activities of faculty in a particular field.

The selection criteria required that the activity occurred within roughly the 1940-90 period, that the faculty involved were "founders," along with external partners, and that the organization had become self-sustaining. Further, time and space limitations necessitated excluding mainly academic and educational associations and organizations, founded for the purpose of providing professional and collegial forums for communication and education. This approach eliminated some important pre-1940 work in organization building in such fields as youth, soil and water conservation, and labor. Those are, however, omissions mainly because of time and space limitations.

The intent for this book was not to present an exhaustive historical account of organization building by university faculty and staff. Given the short time frame, the project was designed to be illustrative of organization building activity across a broad range of fields.

The information gathering process was most rewarding, since it was mainly through personal contact. Once the principals were identified, personal interviews were conducted with each individual or their colleagues, in those cases where the faculty members were deceased. Information in personal files, organizational anniversary publications, published and unpublished historical material, interviews with current executive directors and the current publications of the organizations provided the historical account and the current status of the organizations.

Finding the photographs that would bring alive the people and the subjects was the most difficult part of this project. It was a rare situation where there were appropriately captioned photographs. Once again, personal collections of individuals and their recollections of dates and people provided the bulk of the visuals, with a few photos from archived material and a few from anniversary publications and other sources. It was greatly enjoyable to watch the principals refocus on events that took place some 30 or 40 years ago and identify the times, places and people. Needless to say, the approach is less precise than carbon-dating!

The final step in the process was to get the written material reviewed by the individuals and/or their colleagues for accuracy and to ensure that appropriate credit was given to their many partners, inside and outside the University, who were co-founders of the organizations in focus. Someone said, "credit is infinitely devisable, provided there is some." The faculty and staff included in this book excel at sharing the credit. That is, most probably, what made them such effective organization builders.

Instruction in Maypole Dancing was part of a
University Extension arts program at Milwaukee, 1910.

(Courtesy, State Historical Society of Wisconsin)

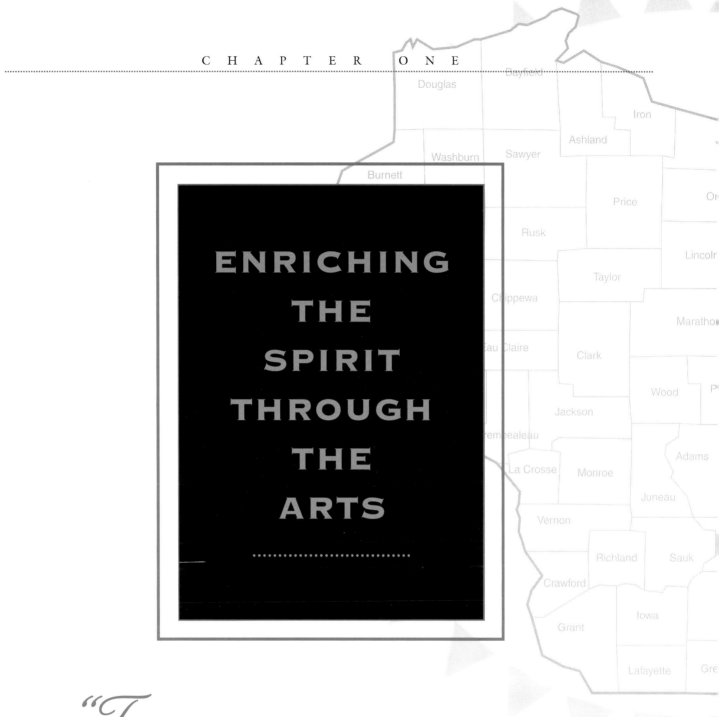

ENRICHING
THE
SPIRIT
THROUGH
THE
ARTS

"The Arts Are for Everyone. Support. Enjoy." Gerald A. Bartell, chairman of the Wisconsin Foundation for the Arts between 1971 and 1990, developed this slogan for a media campaign in support of the arts. He strongly believed that the opportunity to participate in the arts was a universal heritage.

There were others in the state who spent a lifetime helping Wisconsin people lead creative and satisfying lives through involvement in the arts. They were University of Wisconsin professors with vision and energy. They partnered with community leaders and artists around the state and institutionalized the idea that the arts are for everyone. This was the University at its best. It was a shining example of the Wisconsin Idea.

ARTS

The story begins in the UW-Madison's College of Agriculture, as does the bulk of the early work of a University supporting the economic and social needs of society. The story is told that Chris L. Christensen, dean of the College of Agriculture from 1930 to 1943, wanted to put the "culture" back into agriculture and support the needs of rural Wisconsinites to become involved in the creative and liberal arts. The philosophy he established held that culture had to be for all the people of the state, regardless of where they lived, their means or occupations. He believed that culture could be created; that the creative spirit in people needed to be discovered, nurtured and supported.

THE WISCONSIN RURAL ARTS PROGRAM

ean Christensen hired an artist-in-residence at the College of Agriculture, supported through a five-year grant of $4,000 per year from the Brittingham Estate. John Steuart Curry's tenure as artist-in-residence started in 1936 and was the beginning of the Wisconsin Rural Arts Program.

Aaron Bohrod (far right) at a 1968 Mt. Horeb School Workshop

This was the foundation upon which Robert Gard and others would build in the 1940s. Writers, musicians, painters, actors and other artists would emerge from the countryside and the cities, and share their creativity with the broader community. The emotional and physical strains of World War II would slowly fade.

Grace White writes in her historical account titled, *Cooperative Extension in Wisconsin: 1962-1982,* that the artist-in-residence appointment was unique in the nation. It was the first such appointment in the arts at a university. Following Curry, Aaron Bohrod became the second artist-in-residence in 1948, serving in that role until his retirement in 1974. Dean Christensen and John Curry initiated a rural art show in 1940 to showcase the work of rural artists. UW-Madison rural sociologist John Barton served as coordinator of the first Rural-Farm Art Show which featured work from 16 artists. Over the many following years, hundreds of rural artists displayed their paintings at the annual show held on the UW-Madison campus.

James Schwalbach assumed the lead responsibility

of the rural art program in 1945 as the Extension arts and crafts specialist in the UW-Madison Department of Rural Sociology. Schwalbach was a key figure in organizing rural artists and reaching youth and adults through his WHA "Let's Draw" program, as well as through workshops and exhibits in fairs and community art shows.

Schwalbach and his colleagues Kenneth Kuemmerlein and Jane Graff, both Extension specialists, offered regional workshops to reach the adult artists. According to Grace White, "the workshops provided the medium for obtaining nearly 200 regional paintings to be displayed for one month at the Wisconsin Center in Madison."

The Wisconsin Rural Art Association had been started in the 1930s as the official organization for regional arts, co-sponsored by Cooperative Extension and local artists. It was a vehicle for Extension to reach local artists and for them to showcase their talents.

Sometimes the local interest was so strong that local associations would also be formed. Ken Kummerlein is credited with coordinating these local groups with the Wisconsin Rural Art Association to assure program continuity. When Ken Kuemmerlein retired in 1982, Wisconsin's regional art program had achieved national recognition. It was held up as an example to stress the importance of Cooperative Extension support for the cultural arts.

The Wisconsin Rural Art Association became the Wisconsin Rural Artists Association in 1954 and the Wisconsin Regional Artists Association, Inc. (WRA) in 1982. Professor Leslee Nelson replaced Ken Kuemmerlein in 1982 and continued the tradition of attending each Regional Workshop until 1986. When the program was threatened with budget cuts in 1986, impassioned letters from members of the association convinced then Chancellor Patrick Boyle to maintain the program. Today, there are nine to fifteen workshops around the state, involving about 500 artists. A state conference and exhibit day are held each September. The WRAA Board selects 24 paintings for an exhibit that travels to 20 Wisconsin cities. In 1997 an endowment fund was established as a memorial to Ken Kuemmerlein, to continue the regional arts program he loved and nurtured.

All-State Meeting at Green Lake, Wisconsin, September 7-10, 1949. Bottom row: Russ Robinson, Marian Smith, Myra Adkins, Mrs. Viking Ander. Top row: Paul Knoke, Edward Kamarck, Robert Gard, Faith Oemig, Mrs. Anna Gensman. (UW Archives)

THE ROBERT E. GARD ERA

*I*n an article written for the 25th anniversary publication of the Rhinelander School of the Arts, Madison-based writer John H. Dunn describes Bob Gard as "The Idea Man for Wisconsin."

Gard was a man who had ideas on what ought to be and went ahead to make them happen. He joined the University of Wisconsin faculty in 1945 after researching, teaching and writing in Canada and New York. The focus of his work was folklore. Dean Christensen knew of Gard's work at Cornell University, where he taught play writing. The Kansas native seemed uniquely suited to develop a grassroots literary and artistic movement in Wisconsin. Christensen couldn't have been more right in his judgement.

THE WISCONSIN IDEA THEATER

The Wisconsin Idea Theater's "Hodag!" being rehearsed for its 1965 European tour. (UW Music Archives).

*G*ard's primary interest when he arrived in Wisconsin was the stage. So, the "Idea Man" started the Wisconsin Idea Theater in 1945. This institution achieved major success in encouraging Wisconsin playwrights to produce regional drama in community theaters. By the mid-1960s the Wisconsin Idea Theater was offering two full-length musicals written for it. The self-supporting shows were bringing top quality theater to the door-step of Wisconsin citizens. The Extension Service 1965 Annual Report indicates that the summer musicals played to more than 50,000 people in over 70 performances over a three-year period.

David C. Peterson was a protege of Bob Gard and is now emeritus professor of theater arts in the Department of Continuing Education in the Arts at UW-Madison. Peterson combined his backgrounds in choral and orchestral music and drama with his deep interest in Wisconsin history and

lore. His 35 musical shows were presented through the Wisconsin Idea Theater in the 1960s, followed by two decades of presentations by the

Heritage Ensemble. In the best of the Gard tradition, Professor Peterson and his performers based their work on local history and folklore, dramatizing Wisconsin's colorful heritage. The tradition continues today with the American Folklore Theater.

Professor Peterson was the 1993 winner of the Robert E. Gard Wisconsin Idea Foundation's Award for Excellence. His biographical statement for this award estimates that more than one million people have viewed his productions in every corner of the state.

The 4-H drama program was another offshoot of Extension's cultural arts influence. By the mid-1960s, thousands of young people were participating in writing, staging, acting, producing or directing 4-H plays in their county, district or state festivals. For almost two decades this work was led by Helen O'Brien. Under O'Brien's leadership, drama workshops with professional resource people were being organized by county Extension youth agents, to develop skills and understanding of theater arts among 4-H members and leaders. Upon O'Brien's retirement in 1982, Joan Lazarus was

The "discovery of The Hodag". This 1895 photo was staged by Gene Shepard (far right with the pole), the famed Rhinelander prankster who created the Hodag Myth, alive and well in Rhinelander today. Shepard's career as a Northwoods character was the basis for Dave Peterson's musical, Hodag! in 1964. (UW Music Archives).

appointed to work on 4-H drama programs.

The 1965 Extension Annual Report also notes that, with guidance from the Wisconsin Idea Theater, more than 100 community theaters were working on special drama projects.

The Wisconsin Idea Theater lost its preeminence in the 1970s, when UW-Extension shifted resources to other priorities.

Numerous theaters and theater associations filled the void created by the loss of this important arts institution. The UW-Madison department of Continuing Education in the Arts (now the Department of Liberal Studies and the Arts) has continued educational support for theater arts based on contemporary needs and demands, with leadership from Professors Dave Peterson, Harv Thompson and Joan Lazarus.

Writing team for "How Now Sacred Cow?", a satirical revue poking fun at Wisconsin politics. Wisconsin Idea Theater, 1966. Left to right: Tish De Zonia, Bob Browal, Dave Peterson (seated), Irene Conners, Bob De Zonia. (UW Music Archives).

WISCONSIN REGIONAL WRITERS ASSOCIATION

The first few years of Professor Gard's tenure in Wisconsin were devoted to directing the Wisconsin Idea Theater and planning a statewide cultural outreach program. The rural artists had the Wisconsin Rural Art Program, through the earlier work of Professor John Barton and John Steuart Curry of UW-Madison. This program became the Wisconsin Rural Artists Association in 1954 and still exists today. The Wisconsin Idea Theater provided the mechanism for rural playwrights to nurture and showcase their talents.

It was time for the Idea Man to shift his energies in support of writers of poetry and prose.

Helen C. Smith relates the story of nine original neophytes (eight women and an 18-year-old man) who met with Professor Gard in June 1948 to talk about rural arts in Wisconsin. In a 1973 article celebrating the 25th anniversary of the Wisconsin Regional Writers Association, Smith credits Gard with helping to inspire

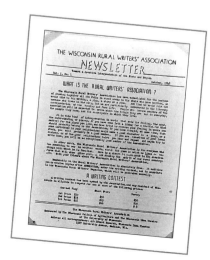

First Wisconsin Rural Writers' Association Newsletter. October 1948. (UW Archives).

the idea for the association during those June conversations. She writes, "The seed sown in June ripened in October, and the Wisconsin Rural Writers Association was officially launched. In February, 1953, it was decided to incorporate. Among those who signed the formal corporate documents were a retired school teacher, Fidelia Van Antwerp, who led the organization for eight years; Professor Edward Kamarck of UW-Extension; and myself."

In less than a year, the Wisconsin Regional Writers Association had grown to 500 members. Replacing the word "rural" with "regional" broadened the association by cancelling the distinction between rural and urban.

Elayne Clipper-Nelson of Portage, President of the Regional Writers Association since 1992, indicates that the membership has been discussing dropping the word regional from the title, but have not agreed upon a suitable replacement yet. The Association has a membership of around 800 now, with members from 10 or more states beyond Wisconsin. The Regional Writers Association will celebrate its 50th anniversary in 1998. Professor Gard would have been pleased with the harvest made from the seeds he helped plant in 1948.

COMMUNITY ARTS COUNCILS

*I*n 1966, the National Endowment for the Arts awarded its first grant for development of the arts in small communities. The three-year grant was awarded to the Office of Community Arts Development, with the Wisconsin Idea Theater of University Extension and the UW-Madison. The grant was aimed at discovering ways to develop greater interest and participation in the arts in communities of 10,000 or less. The Idea Man was on the move again.

Professor Gard selected five Wisconsin communities in which to conduct pilot research—Portage, Waupun, Rhinelander, Spring Green and Adams-Friendship. The pilot projects helped determine what worked and what failed in generating community interest in the arts, and culminated in a national

First Lady Lady Bird Johnson at the opening of the Gard Theater, Spring Green, 1967. Robert Graves behind Mrs. Johnson. Bob Gard, right corner.(Wis. State Journal Photo Archives).

plan entitled, The Arts in the Small Community.

Actually, the idea for the grant proposal and the focus on the local arts council as a vehicle for community involvement were based on the Uplands Arts Council of Spring Green, founded by Gard's friend and lifetime ally, Robert Graves. The local arts council was an idea that proved effective in the pilot communities. In addition to the Uplands Arts Council in Spring Green, the Adams County Arts Council, the Waupun Area Arts Council, and the Rhinelander Arts Council were early successful examples of this idea. As with most initiatives of this kind, each had a community leader with vision and passion behind them — Bob Graves in Spring Green, Harold LeJeune in Adams County, and Cornelia Hull in Waupun.

Of the original pilot councils, the Rhinelander Arts Council, had a broader base of local leadership (including June Eastabrook, Cedric Vig, Jim Caldwell, Warner Bump, Dorothy Guilday and Jack Powers) and survives today as a strong arts organization. The Council is now the Northern Arts Council, an umbrella organization that coordinates and supports a variety of arts activities in Northern Wisconsin. The Rhinelander School of the Arts remains a priority, but the Council provides funding to writers and artists, funds residencies for writers and poets, and awards scholarships to School of the Arts students in the names of Professor Robert Gard, Dr. Warner Bump, its first president and a prominent Rhinelander physician, and Dorothy Guilday, an English teacher who was a local civic leader devoted to the arts.

Bob Graves and numerous other Spring Green community leaders were to play a continuing role in arts development. Bob Graves and the Madison-based staff traveled with Gard across the state, promoting community involvement in the arts. In partnership with Bud Keland, Rudy Kramer and Dave Peterson, Graves established the Gard Theater in Spring Green in 1967. He invited the Robert E. Gard Wisconsin Idea Foundation, which Professor Gard revived in 1981 after his retirement, to headquarter at his historic farm, Aldebaran, in Spring Green.

Both Gard and Graves believed that community involvement in support of the arts would bring business and Spring Green confirmed their belief. The large and varied artists colony there, which includes musicians, painters

Bob Gard's Durable Magic

Wisconsin has lush forests, rolling hills, rambunctious rivers and breathtaking sunsets. And it has Robert Gard.

While some see history writ in bold deeds of famous people, this soft-spoken scholar looks for clues in the lives of ordinary folk.

Their memories, their legends, their traditions, he believes, tell us as much about ourselves and our culture as any dry recitation of landmark events.

Gard — author, playwright, teacher, champion of the arts — has been celebrating the lore and magic of Wisconsin s people for almost four decades. Officially, he retires this month as a professor at the University of Wisconsin-Extension. But the idea of Bob Gard retiring is as absurd as the idea of the Ridgeway Ghost stealing quietly into the night.

He will still be writing, nurturing local arts projects through the work of his fledgling Robert E. Gard Wisconsin Idea Foundation, and listening to Wisconsin folk tell their stories.

His gentleness and humility, his deep love for the state and its people, and his commitment to preserving human history with dignity and affection, have already left a lasting imprint on our cultural landscape. Bob Gard is one of Wisconsin s most durable natural resources. Long may he thrive.

(Editorial in *The Capital Times*, June 5, 1981)

and the dramatists of American Players Theater, to name a few, has stimulated the local economy. Since 1960 the number of lodging rooms has increased from 10 to approximately 270, a simple statistic that illustrates the power of the arts to improve the quality of community life and the economy.

THE RHINELANDER SCHOOL OF THE ARTS

The School of the Arts (SOA) in Rhinelander offered its 34th annual program in July 1997. Its founder, Professor Gard, called it "a dream come true" when this successful arts organization celebrated its 25th anniversary in 1988.

Back in 1963, when it was suggested that he consider starting a school for writers and artists somewhere in the north woods, Bob Gard thought the idea had merit. He had taught at the Banff School of the Arts in Alberta, Canada in the early 1940s, and had watched that small organization become a national Canadian institution. The other projects he had initiated during some fifteen years in Wisconsin were going strong. It was time for the Idea Man to be a catalyst for new ventures in support of the arts.

He consulted his good friend L.G. Sorden, at one time the agricultural agent in Oneida County. Sorden, another Idea Man, suggested Rhinelander as the site without hesitation. He had helped start the Logging Museum in Rhinelander and the City of the Hodag was his favorite place. It had a long-standing and successful Extension program, housing one of the very first agricultural agents in the nation.

There was something else special about Rhinelander — the team of Cedric Vig and Dorothy Guilday. When Gard approached the Rhinelander School Board with the idea of a summertime writing and arts program, Superintendent of Public Schools Cedric Vig offered the use of the Rhinelander High School. Dorothy Guilday, a junior high English teacher, was the behind-the-scenes coordinator and on-site miracle-maker. Vig and Guilday continued their devoted personal leadership over the years, helping

A Wisconsin Idea Theater Company arriving to spend the summer at Door County's Peninsula State Park in 1972. About that time these groups became known as the Heritage Ensemble and continue to the present, now known as American Folklore Theater. (UW Music Archives).

expand the SOA from 50 students in 1964 to over 300 students from across the nation and several foreign countries during its 25th anniversary year. The faculty grew from six to 28 during the same period.

The local support network of financial resources, scholarships and volunteers was credited by founder Gard for much of the school's success. The Northern Arts Council, for example, continues to be a major supporter and contributor. It is such local support that not only helps make dreams come true, but also nurtures and helps them continue to grow.

The School of the Arts is now directed by Professor Harv Thompson, chair of UW-Madison/Extension's Department of Liberal Studies and the Arts. What started as a small number of writing classes for adults in 1964 has blossomed to include 80 different offerings in all the arts disciplines and 40 instructors. Professor Gard would be very pleased.

ETHNIC FOLK FAIRS, ASSOCIATIONS AND LOCAL CULTURAL CENTERS

Corrine Rockow and Chris Powers presenting a Heritage Ensemble performance for school children on the banks of the Mississippi at Prairie du Chien.

Bob Gard's life-long interest was to make people aware of their cultural heritage and to record their experiences and ethnic stories.

He was intimately involved in the Milwaukee Holiday Folk Fair as a writer and as a nurturer of local talent. His year in Finland as a Fulbright Scholar got him interested in the Finnish heritage of Wisconsin residents. He helped the Finnish community in Hurley found the National Finnish American Festival, Inc., which sponsors the annual Festival as well as a cultural center and gift shop in Hurley. The National Finnish American Festival, Inc., instituted the Annual Robert Gard Lecture in 1996 to honor his contributions.

Further, in LaCrosse, Rhinelander and Portage, Gard

worked with citizen action groups to establish cultural centers in their hometowns. In the late 1960s he provided guidance and support to western area regional Extension specialist Darrell Aderman and a group of Shell Lake citizens who established the Indianhead Art Center in Shell Lake. Later

renamed the Indianhead Arts and Education Center, this regional institution has matured over the decades under Aderman's leadership to become a regional cultural and educational resource. Shell Lake citizens have continued their partnership with the University of Wisconsin in the arts through UW-Eau Claire and a consortium of UW institutions which includes UW-River Falls, UW-Superior and UW-Madison.

WISCONSIN ARTS BOARD

*T*oday's Wisconsin Arts Board has its roots in the University of Wisconsin s Extension Division and in the work of Professor Gard and his colleagues who were building a strong arts outreach program in the 1940s and 1950s.

The idea of creating state arts councils was a concept being explored by many states in the 1950s. Wisconsin was one of the first to explore the concept but one of the last to create a statutory agency for the arts.

Formal efforts began with the incorporation of the Wisconsin Arts Foundation and Council, Inc., in 1957. The stated purpose of the organization was "to foster the arts by sponsoring research, providing leadership, conducting meetings, exchanging information, lending assistance and giving encouragement and financial support to individuals, groups and communities." Professor Robert E. Gard was its first president.

In 1963, Governor John W. Reynolds, in response to a *New York Times* article labeling Wisconsin a "cultural dust bowl" for failure to undertake statewide planning for the arts, appointed a Governor's Council on the Arts. There was no state funding to support the Council.

In the Words of the Idea Man and Institution Builder

(From *The Arts in the Small Community*)

If you try, what may you expect?

First a community

Welded through art to a new consciousness of self:

A new being, perhaps a new appearance....

A people proud

Of achievements which lift them through the creative

Above the ordinary....

A new opportunity for children

To find new experiences in art

And to carry this excitement on

Throughout their lives....

A mixing of peoples and backgrounds

Through art; a new view

Of hope for mankind and an elevation

Of man...not degradation.

New values for individual and community

Life, and a sense

That here, in our place,

We are contributing to the maturity

Of a great nation.

If you try, you can indeed

Alter the face and the heart

Of America.

Dean Adolph A. Suppan of UW-Milwaukee was appointed chairman and Professor Fannie Taylor of UW-Madison was appointed secretary. The Governor was unaware of the existence of the Wisconsin Arts Foundation and Council.

Suddenly there were two state arts organizations, each struggling without adequate support.

Governor Warren P. Knowles merged the two organizations in 1965 and designated the Wisconsin Arts Foundation and Council (WAFC) as the "official" state agency for the arts. There was some federal money to dispense, but WAFC struggled to support its administrative needs by seeking private funds. There was still no state support.

In 1970 the WAFC dropped the word "foundation" from its title and became the Wisconsin Arts Council. Governor Patrick J. Lucey affirmed its "official" status. Madison businessman Gerald A. Bartell was elected chairman of the board in 1971 and Donovan Riley of Milwaukee, president.

Bob Gard (left) presents composer Michael Torke the first installment of a $6,000 commission from the Robert Gard Wisconsin Idea Foundation for an orchestral composition (August 1, 1985). (Source: Foundation/Pat Blankenburg).

A conference featuring nationally prominent speakers, supported by the Johnson Foundation of Racine, drew the attention of the Governor and other politicians to the arts. After two decades of stress and frustration, an official state agency to oversee arts development was created in the budget bill of 1972. The Wisconsin Arts Board had 12 members and a modest budget. All authority was transferred to the Board and Jerry Bartell was named its first chairman.

Bartell later reactivated a private non-profit membership organization which evolved in 1977 into the Wisconsin Foundation for the Arts, Inc., and continues today as a strong advocate for the arts under the leadership of his son, Jeffrey Bartell. The Foundation sponsors the "Governor's Awards in Support of the Arts" to honor individuals and institutions for supporting the arts in their communities.

Jerry Bartell's background in broadcast media led to the development of a strong campaign to gain broader public recognition for the arts. The slogan "The arts are for everyone. Support. Enjoy!" became a powerful message. State appropriations in support of the arts increased steadily following the first appropriation in 1972.

The Wisconsin Arts Board is now a part of the Wisconsin Department of Tourism. It has a budget of over $2.5 million through a state appropriation and a grant of over $400,000 from the National Endowment for the Arts. The Board is working to change its focus from just a grants-making organization to one which serves local arts organizations. According to Dean Amhaus, former Executive Director of the agency, "the Board has taken the Gard vision and implemented it. We started developing local art councils in 1992. There are over 70 local councils now." The Board's ten staff members now work on behalf of local arts agencies and allocate the funds to them.

Bob Gard would have been very pleased with the success and the vision of the Wisconsin Arts Board. "Get the money to the people and let them make the arts," that was Bob Gard s philosophy.

THE ROBERT E. GARD
WISCONSIN IDEA FOUNDATION

Bob Gard, the "Idea Man" with his favorite tool. 1988. (Source: School of the Arts at Rhinelander 25th Anniversary Book.)

The last institution Bob Gard built and left to the Wisconsin arts community is the Robert E. Gard Wisconsin Idea Foundation.

The Foundation was an outgrowth of the Wisconsin Idea Theater Foundation, which Gard incorporated in 1962 to supplement University of Wisconsin support to the Theater.

Gard's strong relationships with community leaders around the state over decades of building the Community Arts Program through UW-Madison and UW-Extension became pivotal in this new initiative. As Bob Gard was working to revive the Foundation, Bob Graves offered him use of the Aldebaran Farm. The 135-year-old homestead was once owned by James Lloyd-Jones, a favorite uncle of Frank Lloyd Wright, and later by Wesley Peters, son-in-law of Wright and chief architect of Taliesin Associated Architects.

The farm housed Aldebaran Associates, a land use planning group, where Graves was one of the principals. The invitation to the Wisconsin Idea Foundation to make Aldebaran its headquarters was gratefully accepted by Gard. He is quoted as saying that Bob Graves was their link with reality; not much could be achieved without the property.

More than 200 people came to the farm to inaugurate the Wisconsin Idea Foundation on July 11, 1981. A reception on the lawn was followed by a walk to the Unity Chapel, on the grounds of the Jones-Wright family cemetery. The evening program featured harp music by Karen Atz, tributes by state and university officials, and a recognition dinner in the Great Barn designed by Wesley Peters. Two nationally known artists, Bill Armstrong of Missouri and Francis Myers of Wisconsin, exhibited their work in the Great Barn for the occasion.

The board of directors of the Wisconsin Idea Foundation started with Gard as president, and John Bruemmer, Toby Sherry, Paul Hassett, John Whitmore, Janet Kooiman and Georgianne Yost as directors. The Foundation sponsored art exhibits, handicraft exhibits, folk dances, meetings of arts organizations, artists-in-residence programs, international conferences and other art events during its early years.

The Foundation inaugurated an annual Award for Excellence in 1990. It continues to honor the contributions of Bob Gard, the Idea Man, to Wisconsin through this annual award.

THE EMMETT SARIG ERA

*E*arly history of Cooperative Extension music education goes back to the turn of the century and includes legends such as Edgar "Pop" Gordon of the UW-School of Music who offered the "Journeys in Music Land" program on WHA for many decades.

Professor Emmett Sarig, founder of the University of Wisconsin Extension Music Department, came to Wisconsin on a one-year contract as UW Band Director following a tragedy. Ray Dvorak, famed director of the UW Bands, had lost his arm in a 1948 train accident. Sarig was the temporary replacement. Fortunately, upon Dvorak's return, he stayed on to build the Extension Music Department, including the Wisconsin String Development Program.

Professor Sarig directed the Summer Music Clinic for 11 years, and established the Midwinter Music Clinic (forerunner of the State Music Convention.) Together with Professor Dick Wolf, he coordinated the first State Music Convention, which brought together various music educators associations. He developed a national Youth Music Project which brought rock musicians and music educators together to better understand the "rock phenomenon" and its relationship to music education.

Professor Emmett R. Sarig, the visionary founder of UW-Extension's Music Department and the father of the Wisconsin String Development Program.

Ed Hugdahl joined Sarig in 1952. Together they ensured that Wisconsin residents would have every opportunity to enjoy music.

They helped set up county Homemakers and 4-H choruses, as well as state choruses and 4-H bands. They took their music workshops all across the state and taught music sessions at College Week for Women. Although some choral group programs were eliminated upon the reorganization of UW-Extension, Bob Swan and David Peterson continued to offer exciting educational opportunities to young people through the 4-H music program.

Ed Hugdahl focused his talents and energies on church musicians; he wanted to reach the estimated fifteen thousand part-time church musicians in Wisconsin with educational programs. For twenty years he teamed up with Arthur Cohrs of UW-Green Bay and Arlyn Fuerst of the Trinity Lutheran Church of Madison to offer eight to ten traveling workshops each summer, as well as a 3-day summer conference in Madison. He kept in touch with the church musicians through ETN programs in the winter.

WYSO'S Music Directors. (Seated left to right) Marvin Rabin (Founder), James Latimer, Karlos Moser, (standing left to right) David Nelson and James Smith.

Hugdahl still felt that more was needed. The American Guild for Organists had been in existence since 1896, but this association did not include part-time and amateur musicians. To get a broader base of organists and attract the smaller church musicians, Hugdahl helped found the Association of Church Musicians in the early 1980s. The Dane County branch of the American Guild for Organists supported the move. The Association of Church Musicians incorporated a few years later and now has a membership of over 100 churches with 400 church musicians.

WISCONSIN YOUTH SYMPHONY ORCHESTRAS

One of the most significant contributions of Emmitt Sarig was to build a constituency of music professionals that would push for UW support of a strings development program. With the help of Lu Einum (Wisconsin Federated Music Clubs), Roland Johnson (Madison Symphony Orchestra),

LeRoy Klose (Madison Public Schools music supervisor), G. Lloyd Schultz (Department of Public Instruction music consultant), Dale Gilbert (director of the UW School of Music), and other supporters, Emmett Sarig convinced the University of Wisconsin of the need for a strings development program, and identified Marvin Rabin of Boston as the man who could build it.

Conductor Rabin with students. 1967.

Marvin Rabin arrived in Wisconsin in the fall of 1966. He founded the Wisconsin Youth Symphony Orchestra and started the Wisconsin Strings Development Program within weeks of his arrival. Charter members came from 21 Wisconsin communities. Some traveled 110 miles each way to participate in rehearsals every Saturday morning. Parents or school music teachers took the wheel for those who were too young to drive. Rehearsal space was limited, conflicts with other users for rehearsal time were frustrating, audiences were not always as large as desired, and some of the required instruments were not always available. But, they prevailed.

Over the first 30 years, more than 2,500 young people from 104 communities in 30 counties enjoyed the weekly benefits of this program.

WYSO managers: Front, left to right, Karen Richardson, Bruce Matthews, (back row), Mary Jo Biechler, and Dick Wolf.

The Wisconsin Youth Symphony Orchestras is a truly collaborative organization. The board of directors of WYSO is responsible for the organization; they draw on the resources of the University of Wisconsin, which provides rehearsal space, concert halls, office and library space, use of special instruments and, in the early years, personnel. Professor Dick Wolf was the first manager of WYSO, serving for five of its formative years in this position. The Board also draws on a statewide support system consisting of foundations corporations, arts boards and thousands of individual contributors of money and in-kind services. The Parents Association and student members support the organization through fundraising projects.

Emmett Sarig's dream expanded under the leadership of Professor Rabin. In January 1971, the Wisconsin Junior Youth Symphony Orchestra (since renamed the Philarmonia) was created. A third group, the Concert Orchestra, was formed in 1977, followed by a fourth, the Sinfonietta (strings only) in 1993. In its first 30 years, WYSO's four orchestras toured in five foreign countries, 12 states, the District of Columbia, and communities in 30 Wisconsin counties.

The Wisconsin Youth Symphony Orchestras are going strong. Financial support is at a healthy level. Parents, alumni, families and friends provide a great support base. Corporations, foundations and civic organizations continue to acknowledge the importance of this organization, which showcases the talent of dedicated young musicians, through financial support. The University of Wisconsin is still an important partner in this creative venture.

Emeritus Professor Dick Wolf summarizes the feelings of all those involved in building this organization. He says, "You knew great things were happening. You knew you were changing kids lives."   *WYSO rehearsal*

Marvin Rabin, founder of the Wisconsin Youth Symphony Orchestras, has proudly watched his children and grandchildren perform with the other talented musicians of WYSO over the years. The second generation members of WYSO, children of charter members, have been in the orchestras for some years now. Other charter members, music directors, managers, librarians, parents and alumni constitute a formidable network which will surely keep the WYSO dream alive and vibrant.

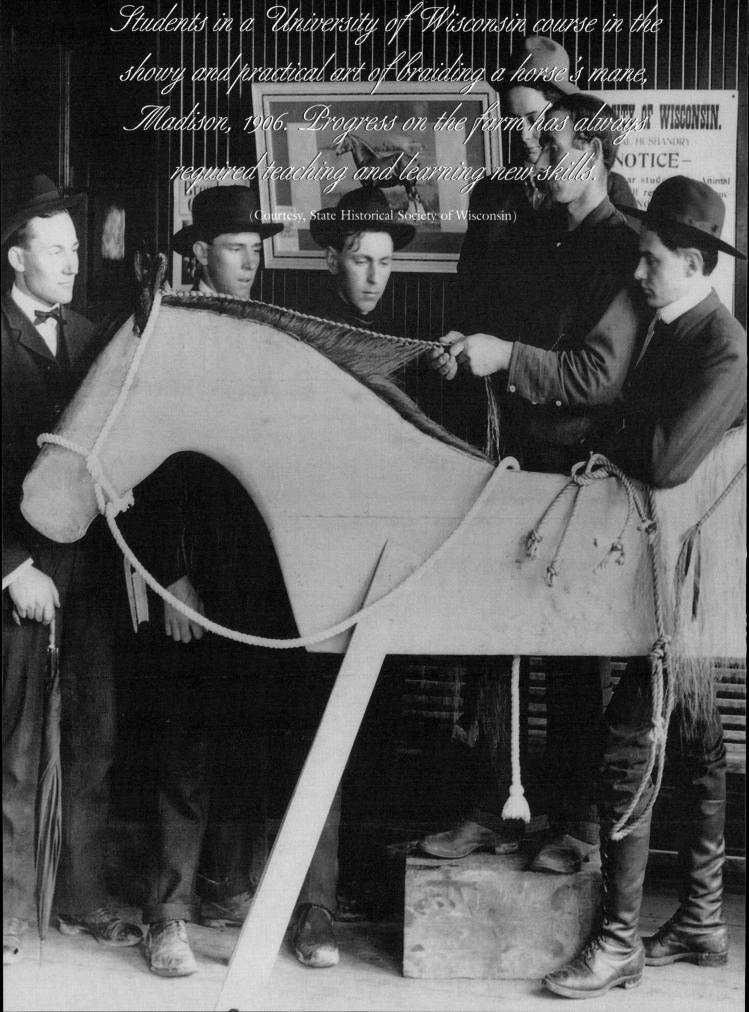

Students in a University of Wisconsin course in the showy and practical art of braiding a horse's mane, Madison, 1906. Progress on the farm has always required teaching and learning new skills.

(Courtesy, State Historical Society of Wisconsin)

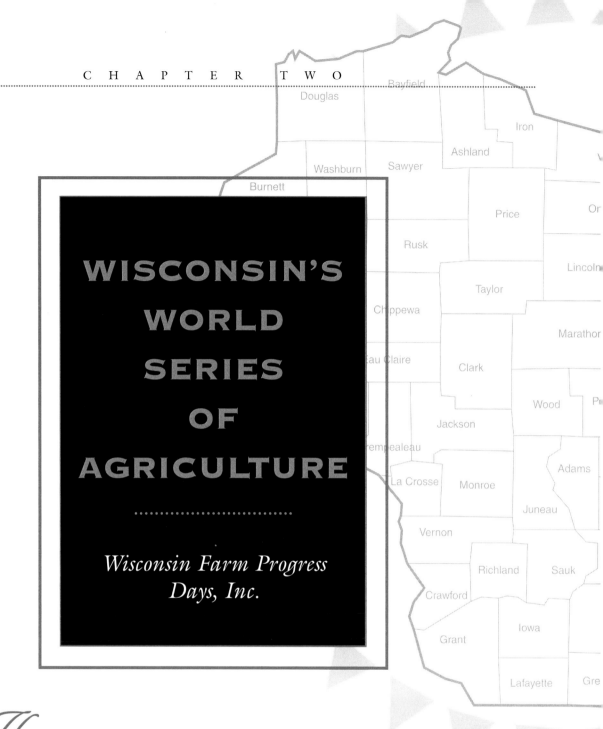

CHAPTER TWO

WISCONSIN'S WORLD SERIES OF AGRICULTURE

....

Wisconsin Farm Progress Days, Inc.

$\mathcal{H}$enry (Hank) Ahlgren envisioned a big farm show, one that could be called the "World Series of Agriculture." He not only realized his vision but the phrase has stuck as a descriptor for Wisconsin Farm Progress Days since he first used it in 1954.

Hank Ahlgren felt compelled to act because farmers were complaining about parking problems on the UW-Madison campus during Farm and Home Week, a large annual event that had been held on the agricultural campus for many years. At the same time, the focus of the Wisconsin State Fair had shifted from rural to urban. While the Fair continued to have an agricultural emphasis, the participation level of the agribusiness community had declined.

Ahlgren acted with reluctance. He knew that, except for parking, these folks enjoyed coming to the campus for Farm and Home Week. He liked having farmers and their families on campus every year. It fortified the relationship between the agricultural producers and their College of Agriculture. It would not be the same off campus. But, it was decision time. And, if he felt it was decision time, there was no stopping Hank Ahlgren, the renowned agronomist who became associate director of Cooperative Extension in 1952 and chancellor of UW-Extension in 1969.

On February 13, 1954, Ahlgren called together a group of agency representatives to discuss conservation field days, plowing matches and land judging programs. The public agencies involved in this meeting were the Wisconsin Department of Agriculture (A.R. Kurtz), CALS Home Economics Extension Service (B. Lee), Soil Conservation Service (M.F. Schweers), Farmers Home Administration (T. Pattison), Agricultural Stabilization and Conservation Service (W.R. Merriam), State Board of Vocational and Adult Education (M.W. Cooper), Wisconsin Conservation Department (L.P. Voight), State Association of District Supervisors (O. Schiffer), State Soil Conservation Committee (F. Patch) and the State Department of Public Instruction (G. Watson). The group decided to form a general committee of agency representatives and selected A.J. Wojta as its chairman.

At the follow-up meeting on March 22, 1954, which was called for the purpose of planning the 1954 Conservation Field Day and Plowing Matches, the group decided to form an organization which could plan such events from year to year and assist local groups in conducting these large field days. Wisconsin Farm Progress Days, Inc. is the result of this decision. The incorporation papers were filed on June 21, 1954 by Arthur Kurtz. Ahlgren was elected chair of the Board, Kurtz was elected vice-chair and Alfred Wojta was selected as the first general manager, as well as secretary/treasurer. Wisconsin Farm Progress Days (WFPD) was institutionalized.

The first organized event this new organization was to hold was Wisconsin Farm Progress Days in Waupaca County in 1954. As luck would have it, more than eight inches of rain fell that week and the show was cancelled. Henry Ahlgren vividly remembers Melvin Laird's car getting stuck in the mud, with a "Laird for Congress" sign atop his vehicle. In subsequent

Merle Schuler of Manitowoc County was the most capable junior level land plowman in Wisconsin. He competed with six other regional winners at the Farm Progress Days in Waupaca County for the top place in 1955. He took first place again in 1956 in Jefferson County. (Source: Ron Schuler)

years, governors and other state and congressional representatives would make a point of visiting this agricultural show come rain or shine.

Since rain flooded the site of the first show, Wisconsin Farm Progress Days has made the rounds of 35 counties in the state, returning to Waupaca County in 1955 and 1978. The 1978 show celebrated the 25th Anniversary of the event. The state map identifies the dates and host counties through the year 2000.

Article 3 of the incorporation papers lists the purposes of Wisconsin Farm Progress Days as follows:

"..to promote a prosperous and permanent agriculture for Wisconsin by conducting, in communities of the state, farm progress days, agricultural contests, conservation demonstrations, machinery exhibits, agricultural tours, educational events, programs and displays, and anything necessary or incidental to the conduct of such activities, which may be conducted in cooperation with other persons and organizations."

This annual outdoor agricultural exposition has remained faithful to its original purposes. The shows continue to "showcase" Wisconsin agriculture, emphasize education based on cutting-edge science, focus on current and new technologies, highlight critical emerging issues, and promote a sustainable and profitable agriculture.

In recent years, Wisconsin Farm Progress Days, Inc. has expanded the involvement of the agricultural leadership of the state in its decisions. Membership on the Board of Directors has been expanded to include an agribusiness sector representative, a representative of the farm equipment and machinery sector, and a producer. "This has worked so well that I don't know why we didn't do it sooner," comments Don Peterson, current Executive Director of Wisconsin Farm Progress Days, Inc.

Dr. Henry Ahlgren, Director of Cooperative Extension, with Governor Gaylord Nelson at the Rock County Farm Progress Days Show, 1961. (Hank Ahlgren files)

Map showing location by years.

WISCONSIN FARM PROGRESS DAYS — THE SHOW

*W*isconsin Farm Progress Days grew out of and replaced the state plowing matches. During the early 1950s, state plowing contests were the main outdoor agricultural events in many states, followed by a national contest in which state winners participated.

State plowing contests in Wisconsin featured field demonstrations and educational programs relating to land management and land use, soil and water conservation, land leveling, pasture renovation and improvement, and farm safety. These were in addition to the main events, which were the plowing contests conducted on level and contour lands. Also, during the 1953 event, which preceded the national plowing matches being held in Wisconsin for the first time, there were displays of farm equipment and machinery, as well as other agricultural products. Featured speakers and entertainment were also a part of the event.

In addition to the 60-acre Tent City, 100 acres are needed for visitor parking and another 250 acres for field crop demonstrations and harvesting, for a total requirement of over 400 acres.

Between 1954 and 1957, a time of organization, Wisconsin Farm Progress Days repeated much of the activity included in the 1953 event. But, interest in plowing contests was declining and the WFPD Board felt compelled to modify the purpose and activities of the farm show.

In 1957, the Juneau County show continued to place emphasis on conservation, but farm demonstrations focused on corn harvesting using pickers, shellers and combines were incorporated and grassland farming concepts were also brought into the show.

In 1958, the LaFayette County show introduced rural recreation activities. The Marinette County show in 1959 added forestry and forest products emphasis to the grassland farming approach.

Each year since 1960, the summer shows have emphasized forages and other summer crops, while fall shows have focused on fall harvested crops. Transfer of research findings, demonstrations of farm equipment and agricultural products, and educational programs for the farm and home continue to be standard features of Wisconsin Farm Progress Days.

Wisconsin Farm Progress Days has grown larger every year since 1954. Today's event includes over 600 commercial exhibitors located in a Tent City exhibit and display area which occupies some 60 acres in the center of the show site. Extensive cropland acreages near Tent City provide farm equipment and machinery companies the opportunity to demonstrate their hardware under field conditions. In addition, participating public agencies, including the University of Wisconsin, are involved in scores of exhibits, displays and demonstrations. Food, beverages and sanitation facilities are available to the visitors during the three-day event, where attendance frequently exceeds 100,000 persons.

Soil and water conservation with strip cropping, grass waterways and farm ponds were showcased in Vernon County in 1963.

Financial support for the show comes from commercial exhibitor fees and donations (cash and in-kind) by local businesses, industries and individuals. Also, the county board appropriates funds for start-up purposes as well as support for the county Extension office—the host county's operational nerve center—to handle the increased work load. Additionally, a nominal admission fee ($2.00) is charged to adults to help keep the venture solvent. The total out-of-pocket costs for the event in the early 1950s was between $4,000 and $8,000. Today's show costs exceed $500,000. Any funds remaining in the host county's WFPD treasury after all expenses have been paid are invested in agriculturally-related projects in the county in keeping with the educational purpose of Wisconsin Farm Progress Days.

A special feature of WFPD is the Progress Pavilion featuring University specialists and agency staffs.

New Feature--recreation and water management. Man-made Yellowstone Lake. La Fayette County, 1958.

The philosophy of the WFPD, Inc. Board of Directors in financing the show is very much in line with Henry Ahlgren's original vision for the event. He wanted the show to be self-sustaining, relying on commercial exhibitor fees and local contributions. He recalls repeatedly being asked by governors and legislators if they should include a line item in the state budget to support Farm Progress Days. He always refused, firm in his belief that the show would sustain itself in other ways.

The formula for success of Wisconsin Farm Progress Days has not changed over the past 44 years. It remains a cooperative undertaking involving the WFPD, Inc. Board of Directors which brings together state and federal agencies, agribusiness and industry representatives, the county board of supervisors of the host county, hundreds of local volunteers who give freely of their time and energies, and the host family(s) who take great pride in representing the agriculture of their county. All of these, working together, are partners in making the show a success. Truly, farmers and their families and other agricultural residents of the host county own the show. Thus, Wisconsin's "World Series of Agriculture" maintains its prominence among farm shows in the nation.

HENRY AHLGREN — COALITION BUILDER

*B*orn in Minnesota, Hank Ahlgren grew up on a dairy farm in Polk County, Wisconsin. He held three degrees from the University of Wisconsin-Madison and conducted extensive research in the areas of pasture and forage crops. He served as chair of the UW-Madison Agronomy Department between 1949 and 1952. He was appointed associate director of the Cooperative Extension Service in 1952 by Dean Rudolf Froker and chancellor of the University of Wisconsin-Extension in 1969 by President Fred Harvey Harrington.

While Hank Ahlgren received numerous national and international honors for his science, his other gifts made him "arguably the most influential and personally powerful College figure throughout the era," as stated by John W. Jenkins in *A Centennial History: A History of the College of Agricultural and Life Sciences at the University of Wisconsin-Madison.* Jenkins reports that Ahlgren's propensity to see the big picture and to express himself boldly led to his writing the Republican Party platform plank on agriculture in 1960.

The General Manager, Glenn Thompson (left) and Executive Director Don Peterson.

**GENERAL MANAGERS
WISCONSIN FARM
PROGRESS DAYS, INC.**

A.J. Wojta (Agricultural Engineering) **1954-59**

F.V. Burcalow (Agronomy) **1960-62**

Randall Swanson (Agricultural Engineering) **1963-68**

George Wright (Cooperative Extension) **1969-76**

Lynndon Brooks (Agricultural Engineering) **1977-84**

A.J. Francour (Cooperative Extension) **1985-92**

Glenn Thompson (Cooperative Extension) **1993-**

Dr. Ahlgren was a national leader in the Cooperative Extension System. His passion was to direct the resources of the nation's land grant colleges and universities to greater service to agriculture. He was an institution builder, a forceful speaker and a leader of great vision. He connected with every part of Wisconsin agriculture. He could build coalitions which would then become institutions.

Ahlgren revolutionized Cooperative Extension in Wisconsin. He broadened the educational services, upgraded the quality of county Extension staff, and helped put in place the Wisconsin Associated County Extension Committees, Inc. which solidified the county partnership with the University of Wisconsin and the U.S. Department of Agriculture.

He was instrumental in organizing and building the World Series of Agriculture — Wisconsin Farm Progress Days, Inc. — which continues to sponsor one of the finest agricultural shows in the country.

In 1990, besides corn and soybeans, the latest potato harvesting equipment drew a lot of attention.

Clark County Agent Wallace Landry reading newsclips announcing the formation of one of Wisconsin's first rural electrical cooperatives in 1935. Extension farm agents took the lead in organizing the cooperatives that brought electrical power to the countryside.

(Courtesy, Wisconsin Rural Electrical Cooperative News)

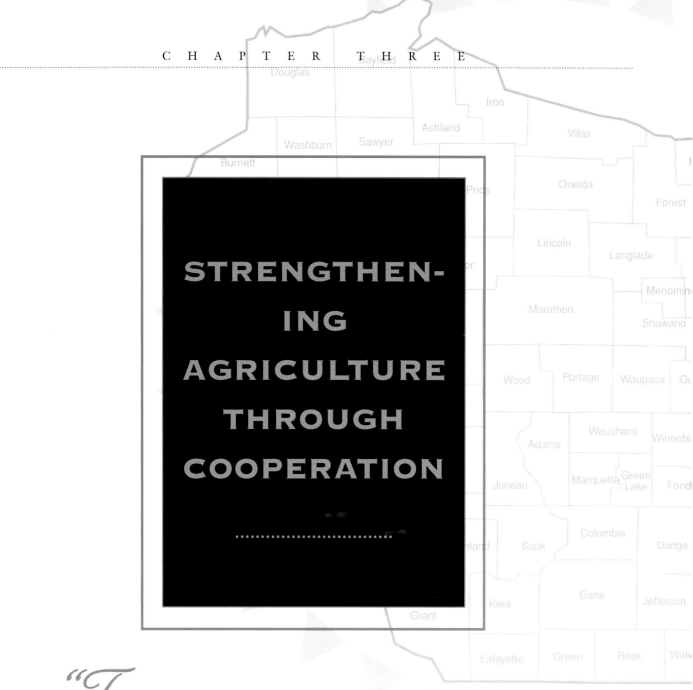

STRENGTHEN-
ING
AGRICULTURE
THROUGH
COOPERATION

"The history of the farm marketing problem in the state and nation, as well as throughout the world, points to the solution chiefly through the cooperative marketing efforts of producers. It is herein declared to be the policy of this state in advancing the general good and public welfare to assist in the organization and development of cooperative associations for production and marketing purposes," so reads Chapter 94, Wisconsin Laws of 1957.

The legislative mandate had caught up with reality. For 30 years or more, county agricultural agents and campus specialists from the Cooperative Extension Service of UW-Madison's College of Agriculture had been helping farmers improve their income through cooperation.

Capital Times headline February, 1960 after the release of the draft copy of report titled, "Dairy Marketing Problems in Wisconsin." Recommendations on price supports, federal marketing orders and, especially, a state milk control program were controversial.

Their work was not always welcome. In many a case, agents and campus specialists were warned to remove themselves from cooperative formation and marketing work. In some cases their jobs were in jeopardy, but they prevailed. They helped farmers build self-help, farmer-owned and controlled cooperatives. They helped with organization papers. They promoted membership loyalty and understanding. They nurtured and supported their young organizations as they matured.

In the 1920s and 1930s, county agricultural agents and campus specialists helped farmers form specialized commodity marketing units in wool, tobacco and sugar beets. There was also significant early work in livestock, poultry and dairy cooperatives. In dairy, Consolidated Badger Cooperative of Shawano and the Antigo Milk Products Cooperative stand out as strong examples of university support for cooperative formation during the Depression Era.

County agent G.F. Baumeister of Shawano County, Superintendent of Farmers' Institutes E.L. Luther, and agricultural economists and extension specialists R.K. Froker (later Dean Froker) and Hans T. Sondegaard of UW-Madison are credited with helping build these organizations. Both of these cooperatives served as models for Manitowoc County farmers struggling to pool their resources in the mid-1940s.

LAKE TO LAKE COOPERATIVE

*I*n March 1945, dairy farmers Henry Binversie and Melvin Lutzke from the town of Meeme in Manitowoc County visited their county agricultural agent Truman Torgerson to ask for help. The county had 57 cheese factories, two condenseries, and several small milk bottling operations. The bottlers were serving only local markets and had not yet instituted Grade A milk. Binversie and Lutzke wanted help in merging their small Hi Point Cooperative with other local cooperatives.

Torgerson had worked with the successful Ladysmith Cooperative Creamery while serving as agricultural agent in Rusk County. He also knew of Marketing Specialist Rudy K. Froker's work in Shawano and Langlade counties. He called Froker to a meeting in May 1945 at School Hill to explain how he helped organize Consolidated Badger and Antigo Milk Producers during the Depression. At the meeting he related their accomplishments to the leading farmers of Manitowoc county in the audience.

A farmer's committee was formed as a result of this meeting and, with Froker's guidance, ideas were generated. While the group was settling on what kind of organization they wanted to form, Froker nudged them to think broadly and consider a natural geographic area, like that between Lakes Winnebago and Michigan, all the way up to Door County. While they brainstormed names for the cooperative, Froker suggested "Lake to Lake." It fit the vision.

In December 1945, Torgerson helped plan a countywide meeting at Silver Lake, near Manitowoc. Froker was there, as were Otto Wirth, manager of the Antigo Milk Producers Cooperative, and T. Christoferson, manager of the Dairyland Cooperative in Juneau. Upon hearing their information and accounts of success, 88 of the 500 farmers in attendance signed five-year contracts that day.

The Door County group at the meeting soon joined. The Door and Manitowoc County Steering Committees embarked on a membership drive. Their goal was 500 members or 10,000 cows in Manitowoc County and 400 members in Door County. Torgerson provided the organizing support in Manitowoc County and Paul Wolski, assistant agricultural agent, was the backbone of support to the steering committee members in Door County. By July of 1946, the membership goals were achieved and formal organizing meetings were held at Silver Lake and Sturgeon Bay.

Organizing Lake to Lake Cooperative in the other counties included in Froker's vision was slow going. There were also the usual groundwork of developing the by-laws and obtaining the financing. A rich story of the hurdles that had to be overcome is told by Torgerson in his book, *The Lake to Lake Story*.

The original Board of Directors, elected in 1946, was chaired by A.C. Murphy. They conducted a search for a manager, interviewed several candi-

Professor Truman Graf at the Council of Agriculture meeting discussing federal milk marketing orders at Kiel. Left to right: General Manager Torgerson, VTAE Instructors Ralph Kramer and Len Turnell, County Extension Agent Ernie Ehrbar.

dates, and hired county agent Torgerson. At age 30, Torgerson changed careers. He managed the Lake to Lake Cooperative until his retirement in 1980 after it merged with Land O'Lakes after steady and consistent growth. He had helped build markets and people through cooperation for over 35 years as President and General Manager.

FORMATION OF WISCONSIN DAIRIES (NOW FOREMOST FARMS USA)

*I*n the summer of 1959, Governor Gaylord A. Nelson wrote to President Elvehjem of the University of Wisconsin requesting the appointment of a Dairy Marketing Committee to study the state's dairy marketing problems and to make recommendations. He laid out the issues he wanted considered by the committee, asked for an initial report at the earliest possible date, and requested that Dean Rudolf K. Froker of the College of Agriculture serve as a special consultant to the committee and to him.

Young professors Truman Graf and Frank Groves, agricultural economists with UW-Madison, at the time of their 100-meeting year, ready to discuss the mechanics and benefits of consolidation.

The Dairy Marketing Committee was chaired by Marvin A. Schaars, chairman of the Department of Agricultural Economics, and included as members Hugh L. Cook, Truman Graf, Harlow Halverson, Willard F. Mueller and William C. Winder. All were agricultural economists, except for Winder who was a food scientist. Dean Froker accepted the assignment as special consultant to the committee.

The committee issued two reports: "Dairy Marketing Problems in Wisconsin" (March, 1960), and "Improving the Efficiency of Dairy Cooperatives in Wisconsin" (September, 1960). The first report made headlines in the state's newspapers through its recommendations on national price supports, federal marketing orders, and, especially, with its recommendations for a state milk control program to improve prices.

The second report, however, had a tremendous effect on the merger and consolidation activities in the dairy industry of the '60s. The report provided the analysis documenting the potential economic and technical advantages that could be realized through the federation, consolidation and expansion of farmer-owned dairy enterprises. It also described in considerable detail the extent of business done by Wisconsin's dairy cooperatives, as well as their organizational characteristics.

Among the important tributes paid by Governor Nelson for the work of the Governor's Dairy Marketing Committee was the following statement: "Full knowledge of the facts is the first step toward achieving solutions to our problems. Wisconsin dairy farmers now possess, for the first time, the essential factual information, coupled with expert technical and economic guidance, upon which they can improve and build a processing and marketing system that will serve them effectively in today's economy." It was prophetic, when coupled with his qualifier that good information was only a starting point for the deliberation by farmers themselves. Timely action was mandatory if farmer incomes were to increase.

Cooperative Director training in Columbia County. Dick Vilstrup standing. 1978.

Most of the analysis and recommendations in the 1960 report on cooperatives were based on data from a 1959 survey of cooperatives by Willard "Fritz" Mueller, Hugh Cook and Robert Clodius. They had clearly documented the scale economies from large scale management and selling. Now the word had to get out to the farmers.

In the course of one year -- 1962 -- Professors Truman Graf and Frank Groves attended over 100 meetings with the boards of directors of the Wisconsin Cooperative Creamery Association and the Wisconsin Creamery Company, and farmer members in the Union Center, Sauk City and Richland Center areas. At these meetings, the UW researchers and extension specialists discussed the economic benefits of consolidation and merger, while Francis Haugh of the Wisconsin Department of Agriculture covered the legal aspects of such moves.

In March 1963, 1700 members of the Wisconsin Cooperative Creamery Association and Wisconsin Creamery Company Cooperative voted to dissolve their existing cooperatives and consolidate into the Wisconsin Dairies Cooperative.

Agents and university specialists continued working with other cooperatives in the area. The Richland Center Cooperative asked for counsel from Extension and the College of Agriculture. Early in 1964, they joined with the Wisconsin Dairies Cooperative. They were followed by Excelsior Cooperative of Baraboo and Kilbourn Cooperative Creamery of Wisconsin Dells. By March 1965, more than 2,800 farmers were processing over 600 million pounds of milk each year in modern plants. Melvin Sprecher of Prairie du Sac served as the first chairman of the board for Wisconsin Dairies until 1976.

There were 1,808 dairy plants in Wisconsin during 1950. The number had gone down to 243 in 1993, according to Emeritus Professor Truman Graf. This massive merger and consolidation activity changed the face of dairy production and marketing. The survivors had increased market power and enjoyed economies of scale. They also shifted from local marketing to state-wide, regional, national, and even international, marketing.

Ashland Experiment Station. Governor P. Lucey and his staff members, Upper Great Lakes Regional Planning Commission staff and UW-Extension staff after a meeting on "Developing the Dairy Beef Industry." Far left: Duane Trader (Ext. Agent), next to him, Gale VandeBerg(Director of Cooperative Extension), fourth from left Congressman Dave Obey, Gov. Lucey, Dick Vilstrup. Far right, county agent Harry Lowe. 1974.

The change continues. A one-day seminar for cooperative board directors in February, 1997, sponsored by the UW Center for Cooperatives in Stevens Point, featured a two-hour segment on mergers and consolidations. Governor Nelson's statement on the importance of good information based on research as a foundation for timely action is as true in 1997 as it was in 1960.

DAIRY HERD IMPROVEMENT ASSOCIATION (DHIA)

*M*ore money from fewer cows and a better living — that is what DHIA has meant to Wisconsin farmers. The story of dairy herd improvement is an important one. But, just as important is the story of an institution which was born in the College of Agriculture of UW-Madison, nurtured by the College and the Cooperative Extension staffs, and privatized to continue its services to farmers in a new era.

The first cow testing association in Wisconsin was formed in Fond du Lac County in 1905. When the Cooperative Agricultural Extension Act was passed in 1914, cow testing associations became a part of state and federal extension programs. By 1917, supported by federal funding, the UW-Madison College of Agriculture had assumed major responsibility for the program and increased the supervisory staff to four.

In 1926, Cow Testing Associations changed their name to Dairy Herd Improvement Associations. Their numbers grew in the supportive environment created by county agricultural agents. By 1948, with the leadership of the Cooperative Extension Service of the College of Agriculture, 58 county-wide Dairy Herd Improvement Associations had been formed, serving nearly 10,000 farmer members having approximately 195,000 cows on test. Fieldmen were employed by each of the county associations to obtain monthly records for each member to show the production and cost picture of each cow and of the entire dairy herd.

There was too much activity, on too many fronts. Some consolidation appeared necessary. It was time to think about a statewide Dairy Herd Improvement Association. The Wisconsin Dairy Herd Improvement Cooperative (WDHIC) was organized under the leadership of the UW-Madison College of Agriculture in 1956. This cooperative assumed the responsibility of setting DHI policy at the state level.

A four year effort by the Dairy Husbandry Department, with cooperation from State Agricultural Experiment Association, Wisconsin Artificial Breeders Cooperatives, and the USDA, resulted in the machine processing of DHIA records. The Agricultural Records Cooperative (ARC) was formed on July 1, 1959 with financial assistance from the Wisconsin AI Cooperatives. By October of the same year, processing equipment was installed in Building T-17 on the College Campus. Within a year, 5,350 herds involving 170,000 cows were on ARC records.

Another important organization was born. Over the next 25 years, the ARC would move to an off-campus location, merge with WDHIC, expand its services, and slowly move away from dependency on the University of Wisconsin. By 1981 there was one, non-voting University of Wisconsin representative on the WDHIC Board of eight members.

During the 25 year transition of combining WDHI and ARC into the new organization, invaluable assistance and leadership were provided by Extension specialists Eugene Starkey, Clarence Olson and Dave Dixon of the UW-Madison Dairy Science Department, combined with support from nearly every Extension agent in the state.

Incidentally, in 1971, ARC repaid the original notes to the AI organizations that provided start-up funding and gave a grant to the UW for research purposes. That is privatization at its best!

In 1986, Wisconsin dairy herd improvement associations were struggling to find solutions to a membership structure which pitted the statewide organization against county organizations. Professor Dick Vilstrup, working with agricultural leader Phil Hein and a highly productive committee of industry representatives, helped establish a new format which met the needs of the small county milk testing units, as well as the statewide record keeping and laboratory service. His leadership was credited with sending the WDHIA in a positive direction and enhancing its ability to provide quality service to dairy producers.

The management and Board of WDHIC continued to expand membership and update services and facilities. In 1993 they joined with 21st Century Genetics to form Cooperative Services International. Under this joint venture and holding company they combined many operations and services and built a new facility at Verona, with service capabilities to dairy farmers throughout the nation and the world.

Dick Vilstrup and Roger Danielson on his farm discussing the UGLRC Beef Project. (Photo: Russ Kiecker, May 1974)

LIVESTOCK MARKETING

*E*meritus Professor Richard (Dick) Vilstrup, agricultural economist, meat and animal scientist and extension specialist with UW-Madison, was given the National Cooperator Award and the USDA Superior Service Award. He was nominated for the Cooperative Hall of Fame in 1996. This was the culmination of almost 40 years of tireless work in helping build and support cooperatives through research and education. He built on the significant work of Professors Fred Giesler and Robert Grummer of the Department of Meat and Animal Science in livestock marketing and partnered with Professors Harold Groves, Dwayne Rohweder, Richard Vatthauer, Robert Cropp, Gary Rohde, John Cottingham and a multitude of others to bring significant innovations and education to cooperatives.

Livestock marketing changed with the development of new cooperative markets for feeder pigs, graded feeder cattle, and livestock with leadership

from UW-Madison/Extension meat and animal scientists in the late 1950s. The new markets increased farm income from livestock sales by providing new channels, increased number of buyers, grading and competitive pricing. A success story was in the making when Dr. Vilstrup joined the team of Professors Giesler and Grummer as a new assistant professor of Meat and Animal Science and Agricultural Economics in 1963.

Harlan Seyforth, Pierce County Extension Agent, Dick Vilstrup, Mert Timmerman, Pierce County farmer, Andy Anderson, St. Croix County Extension Agent. Working on cooperatively marketing meat-type hogs. 1964.

A FEEDER PIG COOPERATIVE

*I*n 1956, when farmers and county agents in Northeastern Wisconsin met with Extension specialists Giesler, Grummer and Rierson to improve the market situation for feeder pigs, they were facing a haphazard pig marketing system. There were no regular market channels, no official grading standards, and no consistent basis for pricing. The group felt they could improve on all of this by supplying high quality animals in quantities demanded and improve prices and profits by organizing a marketing cooperative. The Wisconsin Feeder Pig Marketing Cooperative was born at this meeting.

The Feeder Pig Marketing Cooperative, with Norval Dvorak as its first president, set up its headquarters at Francis Creek in 1957. It started with 427 members from Northeastern Wisconsin, with first year sales of $676,000. By 1963, 8,000 members from Wisconsin and Minnesota were marketing their pigs through this cooperative, with sales of $10 million.

The new system of tele-markets and auctions designed by UW staff saved buyers time and travel expense and was more competitive than regular auctions. Dick Vilstrup worked with the new cooperative while still a graduate student. Others involved in developing this new venture were county Extension agents Elmer Kohlstedt, Everett Olsen, Frederich Dahms, Lyle Atkinson, Dave Williams and Virgil Butteris. Working closely with the UW specialists and county Extension agents were Norbert Brandt and Norval Dvorak from the Wisconsin Feeder Pig Cooperative.

The Wisconsin Feeder Pig Cooperative broke up in the late 1980s and its functions were first taken over by the Midwest Livestock Producers and, later, by the Equity Livestock Association. It was an innovative step, much needed at the time.

We should also note some history on swine research. Early work in swine artificial insemination was done by Professors Grummer, Giesler, Self, First and Vilstrup, working with Tri-State Breeders, Badger Breeders and the Wisconsin Feeder Pig Cooperative. They developed the artificial insemination system and procedures. This work was the forerunner of later work by UW researcher Dr. Neal First, proclaimed as one of the top scientists in the world in 1997.

INNOVATIONS AND ORGANIZATION BUILDING ON OTHER FRONTS

Almost ten years of effort by UW specialists and Extension agents went into the development of graded feeder cattle sales. Specialists Vilstrup and Ed Hauser, working with county agents, helped farmers form effective marketing groups. Statewide expansion in graded feeder cattle sales resulted in the formation of the Western Wisconsin Feeder Cattle Sales at Sparta, Northern Wisconsin Beef Producers at Rice Lake and the Northeastern Cattle sale at Bonduel. The first Wisconsin graded feeder calf sale was organized by a group of producers at Friendship in 1955 under the leadership of Fred Giesler, Vern Feltz, Ed Hauser and Extension agents Lyle Atkinson and Ivan Morrow. By 1963, after organizing marketing cooperatives statewide, the nine sales associations were selling a combined total of 10,000 head for $1.4 million.

In the late 1960s, Dr. Vilstrup and county Extension agents were asked to work with the Farm Bureau to establish the Midwest Livestock Producers. This cooperative, through its pricing, processing and transportation programs had a tremendous impact on farm income. It was soon serving many areas of the state with a volume exceeding $100 million annually. Between 1965 and 1980, the percentage of livestock marketed through cooperative auctions had doubled with the addition of 12 new facilities.

Professors Fred Giesler and Art Pope, in partnership with the Wisconsin Department of Agriculture, had helped start a Wisconsin Lamb Pool System in 1953 with Equity Cooperative Livestock Sales. Extension agents in 54 counties are credited with participating in the establishment of this Lamb Pool System. In 1980, Professors Vilstrup, Pope and Vatthauer, working with Equity staff, helped establish the Cornbelt Tele-Auction in Baraboo. This innovation in marketing evolved within one year from a telephone operation to a computerized service, with sales numbering 80,000 lambs.

Other important associations organized with the help of Professors Giesler, Vatthauer and Vilstrup are the Wisconsin Pork Producers, the Wisconsin Cattlemen's Association and the Wisconsin Beef Council. In the case of the Wisconsin Beef Council, this important promotional organization was started around the desk of Professor Vilstrup, with beef industry leaders John Jenks, Norb Brandt, Norman Christianson, John Craig and Jim Brandemuehl present at the initial organizational meeting in the late 1970s. Later, Extension agents were involved in the elections for the national check-off program, which supports the activities of the Wisconsin Beef Council.

Professor Dick Vilstrup organizing cooperative lamb marketing pools. Mid-1960s.

Another innovation came when Professors Dick Vilstrup and Dwayne Rohweder, working with Richard Voltz from Equity and Norb Brandt from Midwest, helped develop a successful cooperative hay marketing system utilizing protein and quality testing. his system has served as a model for cooperatives across the nation.

WISCONSIN FEDERATION OF COOPERATIVES

*J*n 1963, when Professors Frank Groves, Vernon Schneider and Dick Vilstrup developed an educational program for directors of Wisconsin cooperatives, they worked with two statewide groups — the Wisconsin Council of Agricultural Cooperatives and the Wisconsin Association of Cooperatives. These two organizations cooperated with the Extension specialists in jointly training cooperative directors and managers. This successful combination of educational programs and the opportunity for the leadership of both organizations to work and communicate with each other strongly influenced their decision to merge into the Wisconsin Federation of Cooperatives (WFC), the strongest statewide organization serving cooperatives in the nation.

Emeritus Professor Richard Vilstrup received the National Cooperative Business Association (NCBA) Honored Cooperator Award at the Wisconsin Federation of Cooperatives' annual meeting in Green Bay, 1996. The award recognizes a person's leadership in the betterment of the cooperative way of doing business. With Vilstrup are Tom Lyon, Vice Chairman, NCBA, left, and Rod Nilsestuen, President and Ceo, Wisconsin Federation of Cooperatives.

The close relationship between the WFC and the UW professionals continued through the decades. The Director Training Program evolved into the Director Certification Program. Then a Young Leadership Program was added. Finally, the collaboration produced the National Chairmen of the Board Conference. Dick Vilstrup participated in designing the Wisconsin Cooperative Development Council (now Cooperative Development Services, Inc.), an affiliate of WFC, and he served on the original Board of Directors.

The strong partnership between WFC and the UW continues today through the UW Center for Cooperatives and its director Dr. Robert Cropp of UW-Madison/Extension.

FARM CREDIT ASSOCIATIONS

The guidelines of the 1987 Farm Credit Act created a challenge for Wisconsin's Farm Credit Associations, some 17 Production Credit Associations and 15 Federal Land Banks. They were to consolidate their organizations. Their leaders asked Professor Dick Vilstrup to help them reach an agreement on consolidation. After 40 meetings of a highly productive committee chaired by Richard Wynveen of St. Croix County, and ably mediated by Dr. Vilstrup, the group hammered out a compromise with eight Farm Credit Banks in 1988. This more efficient statewide structure has been turned into a model credit delivery system, saving farmers millions of dollars.

Dr. Vilstrup continues his association with the Farm Credit Banks in retirement. In 1997, agreement was reached to further consolidate to five

Farm Credit Banks. Dick Vilstrup has predicted that the process will continue until there will be three banks in the future.

THE FIRST COOPERATIVE HOLDING COMPANY— COOPERATIVE RESOURCES INTERNATIONAL

The holding company idea had been around for a while and had been implemented in banking and other sectors. But, there had never been a holding company in the cooperative sector. Given the restructuring in the dairy industry, providers of production inputs were being forced to realign and consolidate their operations. Cooperative Resources International (CRI) was designed as an innovative response to the dramatic changes in production agriculture. This structure not only saves farmers money, but also offers future efficiencies in the cooperative movement by combining administrative functions into a single entity while members continue to operate separate cooperatives.

Professor Dick Vilstrup served as a part of a small team to design and organize CRI. The team also included Thomas Lyon, CEO of 21st Century Genetics, Peter Giacomini, CEO of the Wisconsin Dairy Herd Improvement Cooperative, and Twin Cities attorney Ralph Morris. The formation of CRI was a landmark structural model for cooperative organizations. It brought together the business functions of AgSource Cooperative Services of Verona, Wisconsin; 21st Century Genetics of Shawano, Wisconsin; Noba Inc. of Tiffin, Ohio; and Genex Cooperative of Ithaca, New York. It was organized so that similar organizations could be added easily in the future.

In just three years, CRI had grown to 55,000 members, which qualifies it as one of the largest direct member cooperative organizations in the country.

Dick Vilstrup, Truman Graf and Frank Groves, interviewed for this chapter, are quick to share the credit for their accomplishments and honors with UW colleagues in their departments, at other UW institutions, in county Extension offices and with their thousands of cooperators in the private sector. Such is the make-up of cooperators.

*A field researcher points out the effects of
"No Manure" on an experimental plot
at Madison, 1925.*

(Courtesy, State Historical Society of Wisconsin)

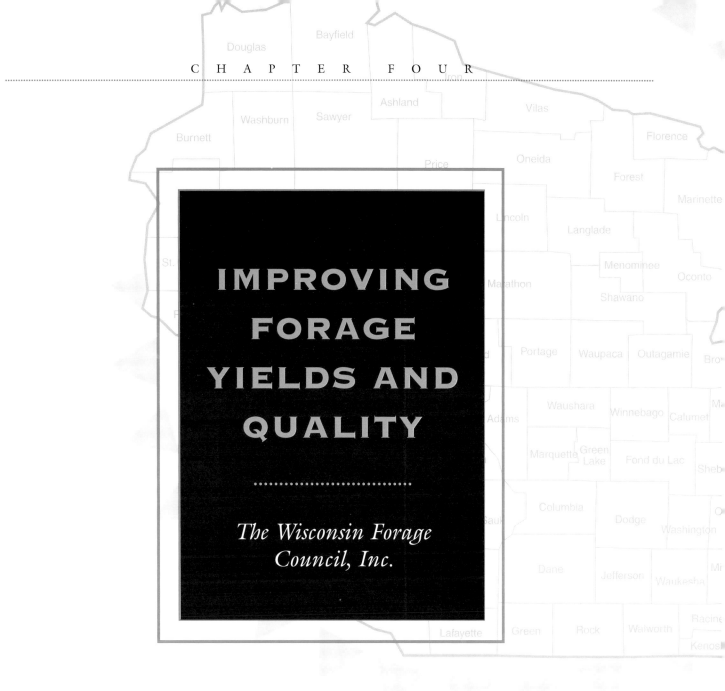

IMPROVING FORAGE YIELDS AND QUALITY

. . . .

*The Wisconsin Forage
Council, Inc.*

$\mathcal{G}$rassland (forage) agriculture has been an integral part of Wisconsin agriculture
since settlement, and of the University of Wisconsin's research and education efforts for
over five decades. Early on, UW-Madison College of Agricultural and Life Sciences
(CALS) researchers were active in the introduction of alfalfa and improved pastures to the
state's agriculture. In 1946, Professor F.V. Burcalow, extension agronomist, took over as
chair of the CALS Grassland Farming Committee. He served in this position until his
death in 1962. This committee developed and conducted a result demonstration
Grassland Contest from 1950 to 1962, in which the feed value production was measured
from natural and improved pastures. The county winners of these contests formed a

Wisconsin Grasslanders Group and worked closely with CALS and county Extension faculty for the improvement of pastures.

The Wisconsin Grasslanders Group slowly disbanded after Professor Burcalow's death. Efforts by Professors D.C. Smith, chair of the Department of Agronomy, and Dwayne A. Rohweder, extension agronomist, to reorganize this group in the 1970s proved unsuccessful. Pasturing for dairy cattle had lost its appeal. It was no longer the "in thing".

Professor Rohweder joined forces with Ewing Row, associate editor of *Hoard's Dairyman* and Greg Krueger, associate editor of the *Wisconsin Agriculturist* in 1975, to explore the potential of a new, formal organization for the purpose of forage yield and quality improvement. If the Grasslanders could not be revived, they'd go at it a different way. They envisioned an organization that would

A no-till drill was purchased by the Western Wisconsin Forage Council to rent to area farm families to encourage them to renovate pastures to improve productivity.

bring together farmers, agribusinesses and agency representatives and invited 200 people for an organizational meeting at Stevens Point in January 1976.

The Wisconsin Forage Council (WFC) was formed at that meeting. The farmers, agribusiness people and agency representatives adopted the articles and by-laws, elected a board of directors composed of three farmers, three agribusiness and three agency members, and elected officers. Edward Staudinger of Reedsville was elected president, Duane Hegna of Baraboo, vice-president, and Dwayne Rohweder, executive secretary and treasurer. The Wisconsin Forage Council was incorporated under the Laws of the State of Wisconsin in 1976.

Activities of WFC during its early years consisted of a newsletter, *Forager*, published five or six times a year; a summer forage field day; exhibits at Wisconsin Farm Progress Days; and annual educational symposia. Each symposium included a trade show in addition to the educational and award programs. Formal proceedings of the symposia were made available to the membership as a means of delivering to them the information presented at these meetings. Attendance at the symposia reached as high as 600. There was obviously a great deal of interest in obtaining the information. Starting in

1987, the WFC began joint sponsorship of the Wisconsin Forage Expo with the *Wisconsin Agriculturist.*

Membership in WFC increased steadily over its first decade. By 1987 the Council had over 1000 members and was the largest forage council and crop commodity organization in Wisconsin and in the nation.

COUNTY COUNCILS

Affiliate county forage councils began organizing in 1980 with the assistance of county Extension faculty. Manitowoc, Sheboygan, Iowa and Sauk counties took the lead. Their purpose was to amplify the dissemination of improved forage production and use technology and to localize the information. By 1989, 29 county councils in 39 counties were affiliated with the WFC. At this time, WFC also became international, with members from Canada and Iceland. County councils were an important factor in stimulating the rapid growth in membership.

Alfalfa variety plots at a Farm Progress Days. The varieties are entered by seed companies and the local forage council plants them. Washington County. 1995.

THE FORAGE PACESETTER PROGRAM

WFC began recognizing farm families for the adoption of new technologies through the Forage Pacesetter program in 1978. WFC has recognized more than 350 families as Forage Pacesetters. These leading farm families were joined in 1983 by winners of awards in the outstanding educator, scientist, agribusiness and agency categories.

THE GREEN GOLD PROGRAM

The Wisconsin Forage Council made great strides in the improvement of forage yields and quality, supported by Dr. Rohweder and county Extension agricultural agents. It organized the Green Gold Project in 1984, assisting farmers in taking yields from a measured area, as well as sampling for quality by cutting. In the first five years of the project, 248 different farm families from 50 counties participated. Green Gold participants averaged

19% above estimated long-term alfalfa-bromegrass yields under top management. Enrollees with top yields averaged 29% above these estimates. The 41 winners averaged 6.2 tons 12% hay and 12,150 pounds milk per acre, or an average of 1,955 pounds of milk per ton of alfalfa forage.

THE MOBILE LABORATORY UNIT

Since the 1960s there had been concerns raised by animal nutritionists and forage scientists about the lack of accuracy in forage analysis to adequately predict animal performance. With the leadership of UW scientists Neal Jorgenson and Dwayne Rohweder, joined by Robert Barnes from the Northeast Pasture Lab, the Digestible Dry Matter Intake System was developed. The WFC encouraged UW animal nutritionists, Drs. W.T. Howard and Richard Vatthauer, to explore the use of the system in ration balancing programs with dairy and beef cattle. Concurrently, WFC was encouraging scientists at the USDA to

Dr. Dwayne A. Rohweder, UW Madison Emeritus Professor of Agronomy Extension-Forages, demonstrating the method of evaluating standing alfalfa maturity and quality to determine the date of cutting near Verona. 1997.

explore rapid, reliable and low cost systems for evaluating forages.

A mobile prototype of the existing forage evaluation equipment was demonstrated at the 1980 Farm Progress Days in Monroe County. Farmers brought their forage samples for analysis, learned about the analysis, and left with the results at the end of the day. There was great excitement because farmers no longer had to wait two weeks and pay high analysis fees.

The WFC Board immediately went into action to obtain a mobile van. They raised the funds by selling $25 shares to farmers, each share providing five "free" samples to the investor. Half the required seed funds were raised from 231 farms. Based on this support from farmers and WFC, Dean of Cooperative Extension Gale VandeBerg loaned $116,000 to purchase and operate the unit.

Additional support came from CALS, which provided $4,500, and from five commercial companies, which gave $9,375. WFC paid the operating funds, repaid the loan and established a replacement fund for the equipment.

The mobile analysis unit went into operation on January 1, 1983 and was scheduled through county Extension faculty. Farmers brought samples for analysis and Drs. Howard and Rohweder were on hand to conduct forage production and use clinics. After hundreds of meetings and thousands of samples analyzed, the following achievements materialized: production and use problems were discovered and recommendations made for change, forage analysis lab productivity doubled, commercial laboratories were assisted to adopt the new methods and perfect their techniques and, most importantly, of the 100 farmers who participated in a study, 73% increased their milk production per cow, with an average economic impact per 50 cow herds of $5,500 per year. A forage testing laboratory unit was added at Marshfield in 1983.

This is collaboration at its best. Through the strong cooperative efforts of the WFC, UW and USDA scientists and Extension agricultural agents, science was advanced, farmers learned to enhance productivity and profitability, and laboratory productivity was improved.

A demonstration of TMR mixers at a Wisconsin Forage Expo. This is a demonstration of using large bales in making rations. (Drs. Rohweder and Howard advised a dairy farmer in Northern Italy to buy a TMR mixer for $50,000. With his 100 cow herd, he paid for the TMR mixer in one year.)

OTHER WFC INITIATIVES

WFC explored the potential of quality tested hay auctions in Sauk County in 1982. At this time, private hay dealers were purchasing excess hay from farmers for resale without a price differential for quality. The success of the Sauk County auction led to Drs. Rohweder and Richard Vilstrup, CALS/Extension livestock marketing specialist, to conduct a series of auctions through facilities of Midwest Livestock Producers and Equity Livestock Auctions using the mobile van. Through 1997, over 800 individual Quality Tested Hay Auctions were held. Cash crop hay producers, as well as dairy and livestock producers, benefited from the auctions. Buyers paid an average of $0.95 per point RFV above full-bloom alfalfa (RFV 100) for increased quality.

In 1984, WFC supported the initiation of the World Superbowl of Forage Quality by Drs. Rohweder and Howard at the World Dairy Expo to

Dr. Rohweder estimating quality in a lot of grass hay by evaluating maturity of seed heads. 1997.

emphasize the nutrition side of the dairy industry. This successful program continues to this day.

The WFC Board has been a big supporter of applied forage research since its early days. The Board funded applied research requests from the staffs of CALS, UW-Extension and the US Dairy Forage Research Center, with the requirement that research findings be discussed at its annual symposia and published in its newsletter. It is hard to improve on such enlightened self-interest.

Dr. Rohweder retired in 1988. The WFC and the CALS Department of Agronomy raised $25,000 to provide scholarships in his name to graduate students in forage and extension, using the interest only. Dr. Rohweder continues to add to this amount. The WFC and Dr. Rohweder continue their successful collaboration in the interest of improving the quality of forages through this fund at the UW Foundation.

THE WISCONSIN FORAGE COUNCIL IN 1997

The WFC turned 20 years old in 1997. There were new leaders, both at WFC and at the UW. Dr. Dan Undersander is the CALS/Extension liaison to WFC. The Council has about 1,000 members and views itself as closely allied with the University of Wisconsin.

The Council's information dissemination continues to be accomplished through an annual symposium that is attended by 300-400 people, with the published proceedings considered to be the most current forage information nationally. Also, statewide field days are attended by 1,000-2,000 people, emphasizing some of the latest technology in forages and offering farmers the opportunity to connect with UW research and extension faculty. The newsletter, *The Forager*, also continues as a quarterly.

Recently, the Forage Council has recognized that less funding is available for applied research. It has established a coordinated demonstration/research program to test principles on farms and summarize and publish the results for its members. The demonstration topics are selected by a committee of the Forage Council and a protocol (with data to be collected) is written by the

WFC PRESIDENTS

Edward Staudinger, 1976-79

Duane Hegna, 1980-81

David Cole, 1982-83

Warren Bottlemy, 1984-85

James Battist, 1986-87

Steven Faber, 1988-89

Rodney Cooke, 1989-90

Dave Schmitz, 1991

Tom Crave, 1992-93

Gary Evans, 1994

John Kappelman, 1995

Dave Tayson, 1996

Bryce Larson, 1997

Special Note: Jean Digney, secretary to the WFC for 16 years. Now retired.

Extension Forage Agronomist, Dr. Undersander. The demonstrations are conducted according to the protocol on farms (one or more per county), without replication, and summarized across sites to develop future recommendations. Field days are frequently held around the trials. This gives farmers a chance to learn the scientific process, to participate in the development of information, and to disseminate the results. This program has shown that the alfalfa seeding rate can be reduced from 18 lb./acre to 12 pounds (saving each farmer $18-24 per acre), that late season harvesting alfalfa reduces yield the next spring, and that frost seeding is an effective method of improving pastures.

Another major recent effort of the Forage Council has been the scissors clipping project. It was recognized that the first cutting of alfalfa is the most important cutting because it is usually 40% of the total season yield and is the one used to refill silos for the dairy herd after winter. Yet, it tends to be the cutting harvested at lowest quality. The Forage Council began a program of clipping alfalfa twice weekly, having the forage quality analyzed and reporting the results to farmers over the radio and by mailings. This effort told farmers when alfalfa had reached 170 RFV and should be harvested. As expected, it has stimulated great interest and has moved first harvest approximately one week earlier into the spring.

Finally, the Forage Council joined with UW-Extension and counterparts in Minnesota, Michigan and Iowa to form the first quality tested hay listing via e-mail in 1992. This was accessed over 4,000 times in the first year, bringing buyers and sellers together. Most importantly, it provided for price determination. The Council provided secretarial service to this innovative project and printed and distributed promotional material.

The recently updated mission statement of the Forage Council says a great deal in a few words: "To research and promote profitable forages, linking producers, educators and industry." All the more power to the Forage Council in its next 20 years.

Dr. Rohweder discussing results of continuing research on the effect of alfalfa quality and dairy profitability with Dr. Dan Undersander, Professor of Agronomy Extension-Forages, at the 1997 Wisconsin Forage Expo near Manawa.

Dr. Undersander has been the UW faculty representative working with the Wisconsin Forage Council since Dr. Rohweder's retirement.

Young pine trees planted in a shelterbelt in central Wisconsin in 1934. The Wisconsin Extension program was the first large-scale shelterbelt planting in the United States.

(Courtesy, State Historical Society of Wisconsin)

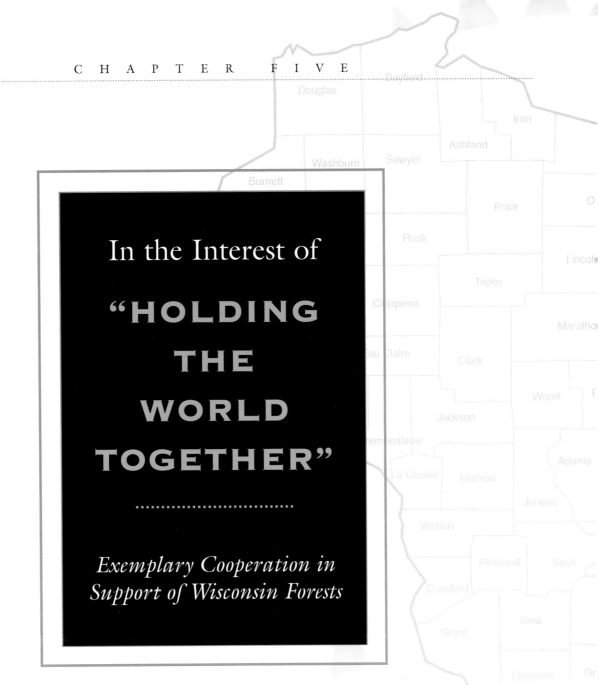

In the Interest of

"HOLDING
THE
WORLD
TOGETHER"

. . . .

*Exemplary Cooperation in
Support of Wisconsin Forests*

*I*nterest in forestry has a rich history at the University of Wisconsin. At the turn of the 20th Century, the noted geologist Charles R. Van Hise was appointed president of the University of Wisconsin. In this capacity he also had a seat on the first board of forestry in the state. His contributions to this renewable resource include co-writing, with the state forester E.M. Griffith, an extensive assessment of the forestry resources and the needs identified with forests, writing a nationally accepted textbook on conservation, and promoting the concept of a federal forest products research laboratory in Madison. He was a champion in the state for wise management and use of renewable resources.

Van Hise also articulated the concept that the boundaries of the campus extend to the boundaries of the state. This combination of outreach philosophy and championing the wise management and use of renewable resources was an established tradition when Frederick B. Trenk was hired as the second Extension Forester in 1931 to start a distinguished career which spanned 30 years. He followed Fred Wilson, who was the first Extension Forester.

There was no University department focused on forestry in those days. Forestry extension work was conducted out of the Department of Agricultural Engineering. The Extension Forester position was also unique in that it was jointly funded by the Wisconsin Conservation Department (WCD) and the Cooperative Extension Service of the College of Agriculture at UW-Madison. Fred Wilson, who had left the university to become the head of the Forest and Parks Division of WCD, was instrumental in establishing the close collaboration of the University with WCD.

State Superintendent John Callahan talking to the school children at the time of dedication of the Laona School Forest, 1928.

Forester Trenk spent his first few years in Wisconsin working to improve land use planning to rebuild the forest resource base in the state. In cooperation with Professors Walter Rowlands and George Wehrwein, Trenk participated in 200 public meetings with local officials. This educational and advisory work resulted in the adoption of the first county rural zoning ordinances in the nation, recognizing forestry and recreation as alternative land uses. During the 1932-36 period, 23

Two generations of Laona citizens were on hand for the re-dedication of the Laona School Forest. C. L. Robinson was director of schools for 35 years and was present at the original dedication in 1928. Two teachers, who were students in 1928, attended, as did their children, present students.

counties enacted rural zoning ordinances, under which about five million acres were closed to future settlement.

During the 1935-45 period, Forester Trenk provided leadership for an intensive Wisconsin shelterbelt planting project. The result was the establishment of some 3000 miles of farm shelterbelts containing over 48 million trees in a five county area in the central sandy plains of Wisconsin.

From his first year at the University, Fred Trenk was a strong proponent of school and community forests as an educational tool in shaping the lives of the young and old. He actively encouraged the establishment and management of 80 community forests owned by local units of government. Together with Ranger "Mac" McNeel, assistant state 4-H leader, he also helped establish 350 school forests.

Fred Trenk left his mark on other initiatives, as well. He initiated the Wisconsin Forest Products Price Review in 1933, the first in the nation directed at owners of timber resources who were interested in finding a profitable market for stumpage and timber products. The Wisconsin Forest Products Price Review was expanded under the leadership of Extension Forester Theodore Peterson starting in 1954, and compiled as separate timber, boltwood and lumber editions in later years. The Price Review constitutes the longest continuous record of price information in the nation. The Price Review was discontinued in 1991 as a result of budget shortfalls.

"Further development of the principles of mechanized tree planting is represented in this original design of a tree planting machine, built by the staff of the Agricultural Engineering Department. A chisel subsoiler, a tree-planting shoe, right and left hand plows functioning as a middle-breaker, a fore-carriage, and a set of tilted press-wheels are essential parts of this machine".

Forester Trenk also left a lasting imprint through the development of the mechanized tree planter. There was an acute labor shortage during World War II and mechanized tree planting was not an option at the time. In Fred Trenk's view, mechanized tree planting was essential for Wisconsin to maintain its reforestation efforts and utilize the state nursery stock. He took his idea of a mechanized tree planter to agricultural engineer H.D. Bruhn. Bruhn and Trenk collaborated in designing a machine suitable for Wisconsin conditions. After the demonstration of the first prototype in 1943, Bruhn built 14 more tree planters by 1944, in cooperation with the WCD.

E.R. McIntyre reports in Fifty Years of Cooperative Extension in Wisconsin, 1912-62 that one machine could plant as many trees in one sea-

Fred Trenk Annual Report, 1943. UW-Madison, Department of Forestry.

Trenk explains tree planter at the William E. Huffman plantation in Biron Village. Trenk is third from the left and on his left is Aldo Leopold. (Trenk Annual Report, 1944).

son as the entire labor force of the Civilian Conservation Corps of the 1930s. Further, he reports that the mechanized tree planter gained nation-wide attention among forestry professionals and implement manufacturers. Within 15 years there would be about 300 of these machines operating in Wisconsin alone. Fred Trenk's contribution, beyond introducing the idea, was to conduct numerous demonstrations (31 demonstrations in 11 counties in 1943 alone), and to publicize the importance of this innovation through interviews with print media.

Finally, and most significant to this book, Fred Trenk left a legacy of institution building which was continued by subsequent extension foresters Theodore Peterson, Gordon Cunningham, Chris Hauge and Jeffrey Martin. In all these activities, cooperation with WCD and later with the Wisconsin Department of Natural Resources (DNR), as well as with industry leaders, was in the best tradition of Wisconsin Cooperative Extension and the Departments of Forestry at the College of Agricultural and Life Sciences at

UW-Madison, as well as the College of Natural Resources at UW-Stevens Point.

CHRISTMAS TREE PRODUCERS ASSOCIATION

red Trenk's 1954 annual report indicates that there was widespread interest in planting Christmas trees due to sustained high prices. Forester Trenk wanted to move with caution. He didn't know what kind of supply increase the market could bear without major drops in price and losses to woodland owners. But, he reasoned that even if the market became extremely competitive, landowners could still benefit by selling their established stands for pulpwood or sawlog.

The planting machine in operation in Portage County. (Trenk, 1944).

Upon the urging of several producers, Fred Trenk decided to canvas the producers on the advisability of forming an association for the purpose of resolving common production and marketing problems. He had 320 producers on file at the Extension Forestry Office. He invited them all to a meeting at Rhinelander in February, 1954. He reports that 100 of them showed up, decided to form an association, and appointed a committee of 21 producers, representing 21 counties, to draft a constitution and present it at the annual meeting of all producers in 1955.

Throughout the year, as the organizing committee met to draft a constitution and elect interim officers, Extension Forester Trenk helped them carry out all their correspondence and other arrangements. When the full body approved the constitution and elected officers at their annual meeting in Bayfield in August of 1954, Fred Trenk was asked to assume the post of Secretary-Treasurer. He accepted.

By November 1954, 80 producers had taken out memberships. Trenk estimated that this represented about 50% of Christmas tree production in the state and 25% of known producers. By the end of 1957, 205 producers had taken out memberships.

Fred Trenk agreed to produce a newsletter for the fledgling association. He had the association make copies for the members and 1,500 additional copies to be distributed through state and federal forest ranger stations, chambers of commerce and the Wisconsin Department of Agriculture, as well as the county Extension Offices. The first newsletter included a directory of members, a checklist of Christmas trees and Christmas greens being offered for sale, and advertising by members. The first two items were free. Advertising space was sold to members at cost.

Forester Trenk also developed an exhibit for the association for the state fair, produced an educational film in cooperation with the UW Department of Agricultural Journalism, and helped the Wisconsin association to affiliate with the national association.

The membership of the Wisconsin Christmas Tree Producers Association had grown to 249 by November 1958. The association was producing quarterly newsletters, arranging educational meetings, collaborating with the U.S. Forest Service to conduct comprehensive studies, and producing reports with valuable information for the industry. They had come into their own.

Dan Anderson Saphouse

Fred Trenk served as secretary/treasurer until his retirement in 1961. The association he had helped build gave him an expanded opportunity to do what he did best — provide demonstrations and education to a group of landowners committed to improve their practices to produce the highest quality Christmas trees at a competitive price.

Upon Fred Trenk's retirement, Dr. Gordon Cunningham assumed the educational advisor role with the Christmas Tree Growers Association. Upon Dr. Cunningham's retirement in 1983, Dr. Chris Hauge of UW-Stevens Point continued in this role with the association into 1992.

The association was on its way. University of Wisconsin faculty in forestry departments could now assume their supportive roles as resource people bringing the best research to the producers.

MAPLE SYRUP PRODUCERS ASSOCIATION

*T*he Agricultural Census of 1950 reported that, in 45 counties of Wisconsin, 500 or more maple trees were tapped for maple sap, with almost 3,000 producers and an annual output of 80,000 gallons of syrup. The value of the syrup sold was approximately $170,000, with an additional $250,000 worth of syrup used for home consumption by the producers and their neighbors.

Forester Trenk saw a dual opportunity in this situation. He explained in his annual report for 1954 that a maple woods could approximate an ideal sustained income from a woods operation. This would ensure that the forest would be retained over a long period. At the same time, new research in processing and utilization of maple sap products by the USDA provided an opportunity for education which would bring better income to producers and expand the industry. Fred Trenk was off to a new program, holding ten one-day institutes for maple producers in January of 1954, with 420 producers participating.

He taught such topics as the economics of production, efficiency of various fuels, marketing, design and use of new equipment. He also involved successful local producers on the program to describe their operations and experiences. At this time there was no producers association to coordinate information flow to producers of maple syrup. So, Fred Trenk volunteered to prepare and distribute a maple producers' newsletter. He had about 1,000 names from four years of institutes. This constituted his mailing list. Special study results on successful production techniques, unit costs and other valuable information were shared through this newsletter.

Farmers at Maple Institutes had opportunity to examine latest type of sap evaporators and other equipment needed for production of high quality syrup.

The Maple Syrup Institutes contributed to providing input to the Wisconsin Department of Agriculture on syrup grades which resulted in more realistic grading of syrups. Also, the idea for a state maple festival came up through these institutes. County agents from Lincoln, Langlade, Shawano and Marathon counties made the local arrangements and solicited samples for competition. The first Maple Festival attracted over 3,000 people. Fred Trenk's office handled the statewide publicity and was represented on the panel of syrup judges.

The Wisconsin Maple Producers Council was established in 1957 from producers attending the Maple Syrup Institutes. The Council was composed of eight members, named by the Wisconsin Department of Agriculture and the Extension Service of the UW College of Agriculture. Each agency also had an ex-officio member on the Council. Once again, Fred Trenk was elected secretary-treasurer.

The Wisconsin Maple Producers Council organized the production of a maple syrup recipe folder, as well as sample bottles of syrup with the Council label to be distributed to attendees at conventions and fairs. The promotion program was showing success. Governor Nelson and Alice in Dairyland attended the 1960 Maple Festival at Aniwa, Wisconsin. Also, menu clip-on cards were being distributed to hotels and restaurants to encourage customers to order real maple syrup for their pancakes and waffles.

Testing finished syrup with a hydrometer, scene from TV movie Maple Syrup completed in 1957.

Fred Trenk continued supporting the Council, producing and distributing a newsletter, organizing ten maple syrup institutes in January, and developing demonstrations in woods management for best sap production until his retirement on June 30, 1961. This energetic and truly committed forestry academic and professional was a vast support system for Wisconsin's forest resource landowners, ably supported by UW Foresters R.W. Abbott and Theodore Peterson. Although Fred Trenk reports desk time in Madison at his University office in his annual reports, it is hard to imagine how he found time to come off the field and make it home. His classroom was, indeed, the entire state. President Van Hise would have been proud.

Dr. Theodore Peterson, the new senior extension forester, assumed full responsibility for supporting the Wisconsin Maple Syrup Producers Council upon Fred Trenk's retirement. Educational and promotional activities continued during Dr. Peterson's tenure. When Peterson retired, Dr. Chris Hauge became the UW representative to the Council. The Council decided to change its name to the Wisconsin Maple Producers Association in 1993. Dr. Hauge, upon his retirement from the University of Wisconsin-Stevens Point in 1994, served as interim executive director for the new association. A full time executive director was hired in January 1996, and then direct assistance for this organization from UW- Extension and the forestry departments at UW-Madison and UW-Stevens Point ended. The Wisconsin Maple Syrup Producers Association stood alone after 40 years of nurturing and support from the faculty and staff of the University of Wisconsin. The baton had been successfully passed from Trenk to Peterson to Hauge and, finally, to the Maple Syrup Producers Association. The University assumed its educational role in support of the needs of the association and its members.

As a final note, we must remember that organizations are not born through the individual efforts of academics and agency professionals. Producers must provide leadership to nurture growth and independence. Milt Thibeaudeau of Luxemburg and Adin Reynolds from Aniwa stand out as state and national leaders among maple syrup producers. They were the real builders of their industry and their association.

WOODLAND OWNERS ASSOCIATION

*T*he Silver Anniversary Forestry Conference was held in Milwaukee in 1953. At the conclusion of the Conference, one recommendation was the need to form an organization of woodland owners to pursue common goals and interests. This idea would stay dormant for over two decades.

There were approximately 150,000 woodland owners in Wisconsin by the late 1960s. They received technical assistance in fire protection, reforestation and some management concerns. Their needs were expanding in a different direction. They needed education, information and technical assistance in marketing and utilization, taxation, capital gains, land use regulations and a host of other subjects.

Most woodland owners at this time were absentee owners from a variety of backgrounds and occupations. They lived in urban areas and owned land in a rural environment for various reasons. They were anxious to learn how to manage their lands for timber, wildlife, recreation and aesthetics. One woodland owner told Thomas Rausch of DNR that he wanted to better manage his woodland "just to help hold the world together."

Demonstration and exhibit on uses of maple syrup in cooking and baking, at the 1960 State Maple Festival in Aniwa.

ORGANIZING GROUP OF WWOA LEADERS

Frederick Braun, Antigo

Gordon Cunningham, Madison

Albert Deppeler, Monroe

Frank Fixmer, Mosinee

Hiram Hallock, New Glarus

Gustav Hirsh, Brookfield

Reinhart Krause, Algoma

Edward Steigerwaldt, Tomahawk

A.H. Wakeman, Lake Mills

Richard Wallace, Kaukauna

David Ladd, Dodgeville

Ernest Brickner, Whitehall

Thomas Rausch, Madison

In 1976, the DNR Bureau of Forestry, under the leadership of Forester Thomas Rausch, decided to capitalize on the U.S. Forest Service interest in organizing private woodland owners. Mr. Rausch obtained a $45,000 federal grant, which was to be matched by state funds. The purpose was to support the formation of an association of woodland owners.

Rausch went to the new chairman of the Department of Forestry at UW-Madison, Dr. Ron Giese, and proposed a partnership to work toward this important goal. Dr. Giese asked Dr. Gordon Cunningham to be the department's representative. Thus began a partnership which would last through the remaining professional lives of two foresters. Also, after two and a half decades of dormancy, the recommendation from the forestry conference of 1953 was about to get some action.

On June 7, 1979, ten of thirteen invited woodland owners and agency and University representatives met at the Department of Forestry in Madison to organize a nonprofit forestry association. The group agreed to a tentative constitution, by-laws, an association name and other organizational matters. Floyd Hovarter of Ashland was appointed acting executive director.

After two additional meetings in July and October, 1979, the board filed the incorporation papers with the Secretary of State on August 30, 1979. Wisconsin Woodland Owners Association directors Hallock and Wakeman joined Dr. Gordon Cunningham on the Educational Telephone Network of UW-Extension to publicize the new association. In the meantime, Gordon Cunningham prepared the first newsletter of the new association and mailed it out in November, 1979.

Even before the first annual meeting of the association, scheduled for August 22-23, 1980, the WWOA Board Education Committee was sponsoring landowner meetings to invite owners to learn better management and join their friends in WWOA. The WWOA Board had also selected William Heikkenen and his brother Carl from Price County as the 1979 Tree Farmers of the Year.

A mailing to 3,300 known woodland owners invited them to the annual meeting. Only 158 attended the annual meeting at the YMCA in Port Edwards in August 1980. But at that time the membership already stood at 804. The first permanent board was elected at the annual meeting.

The primary goal of WWOA was to educate its members and to help them network. Within a few short years, they had taken over the publishing of their newsletter, continuously improving its looks and content. Gordon Cunningham and Thomas Rausch continued their support as technical and educational advisors to the association. They continued to serve on the board, joined by Professors Maurice White and Chris Hauge in later years. After Gordon Cunningham retired in 1983, Chris Hauge assumed the role of liaison to the board from UW-Extension. DNR's Tom Rausch remained on the board until his retirement in 1989.

All these individuals are still active members of the Wisconsin Woodland Owners Association in 1997. Looking back, Tom Rausch remarks that their only failure was to set the bar too high in terms of membership. "We hoped to have 10,000 members by now. It is a real disappointment that we only have about 2,400 members." Others would consider it a real accomplishment, compared to the 804 members in 1980.

The partnership between the Bureau of Forestry of the Department of Natural Resources and the University of Wisconsin departments of forestry has always been exemplary. President Van Hise would have praised the team of Rausch and Cunningham, whose efforts on behalf of this renewable resource helped the Wisconsin Woodland Owners Association through its birth and adolescence. There is still time for the membership to hit the 10,000 mark in the adult years of this organization as the issues facing woodland owners get more complex and strength in numbers becomes imperative.

FIRST PERMANENT BOARD OF WWOA, 1980

A.H. Wakeman, Lake Mills, President

E. Steigerwaldt, Tomahawk, Vice President

Robert Rusch, Rib Lake, Secretary

Frederick Braun, Antigo, Treasurer

Ernest Brickner, Whitehall

Jack Densmore, Madison

Frank Fixmer, Mosinee

Hiram Hallock, New Glarus

William Heikkenen, Brantwood

Floyd Hovarter, Ashland

Milo Tappon, Menominee

Gordon Cunningham, Liaison, UW-Extension

Thomas Rausch, Liaison, DNR Bureau of Forestry

Wisconsin Conservation Department personnel transferring fish from their new "oxygen tank car" into a Wisconsin lake, 1936.

THE WISCONSIN LAKES PARTNERSHIP

In 1968, Wisconsin saw a turning point for management of its thousands of lakes. Prior to that year, the only efforts at managing lakes were limited to fish management by the Department of Natural Resources (DNR), and actions of voluntary lake associations. These voluntary associations had joined together in 1955 to form the Wisconsin Federation of Lakes.

A partnership was formed in 1968 under the banner of the Inland Lakes Demonstration Project. Steve Born represented UW-Extension (UWEX) and Thomas Wirth represented the DNR. This federally funded project was to investigate how lakes could be maintained and to determine who was capable of carrying out long-term management.

Steve Born hired a graduate student named Lowell Klessig to work with the Project. Lowell's major responsibility was to conduct research on existing and prospective lake organizations.

Left to right: William O'Connor, Legal Council for WALD (now WAL), Professor Lowell Klessig receiving the Distinguished Service Award from WALD and the Wisconsin Federation of Lakes, Elmer Goetsch, President of Wisconsin Federation of Lakes (later, Chairman of the Board for WAL). 1986.

The Inland Lakes Demonstration Project experimented with different physical management techniques and evaluated their application. It also recommended that lakeshore communities be allowed to form inland lake districts -- special purpose units of government.

This seed funding from the U.S. Department of Commerce produced the kind of successful results one would wish for any demonstration effort. In 1974, the Wisconsin Legislature created Chapter 33 of the Wisconsin Statutes, enabling the creation of lake districts. It also provided funds for staff expertise in the DNR, which was to provide technical assistance, and in UWEX, which was charged with providing broad organizational and educational assistance. Thus began a three-way partnership between the DNR, the University of Wisconsin, and citizens concerned about lake management.

Lowell Klessig, a sociologist and currently professor of Human Dimensions of Natural Resource Management at UW-Stevens Point, was hired by UW-Extension as a lake management specialist in 1974. His partner at the DNR was, first, Donald Winter and later, Richard Wedepohl.

The early years saw a great deal of organization-building activity. Lowell Klessig developed Lake Tides, a newsletter for people interested in inland lakes. He also solicited the assistance of county extension agents to publicize the program. Klessig, DNR staff and county Extension agents jointly held numerous meetings with lakeshore community leaders to explore lake district formation as a means to protect and rehabilitate the lake.

During the first two years, 1974 to 1976, Professor Klessig provided leadership for awareness and organizational activities which encompassed the following:

◆ Regional conferences in Cable, Minoqua, Waupaca, Waukesha, Crivitz, Green Lake, Rhinelander, Shawano, Eau Claire, Spooner and Milwaukee.

◆ More than 200 separate meetings and hearings with lake associations and local governments in 57 counties.

◆ Information booklets distributed to 20,000 people.

◆ Training opportunities organized for local private and public agency professionals.

◆ Assistance to the DNR in administrative code development and in design of feasibility studies for 60 lake districts which applied for technical assistance.

◆ A media campaign for public education.

Television and print media provided strong coverage of the program and its special events. Editorials lauded the initiative of government and praised enlightened property owners. The program was hailed as pioneering action by the state.

Family enjoying a Wisconsin lake.

Left to right: Lowell Klessig, Wisconsin Lakes Convention Chair, Lisa Conley, 1989 winner of Wisconsin Lake Stewardship Individual Award, Kevin MacKinnon, Representing Town of Delevan Lake Committee, 1989 winner of Lake Stewardship Group Award.

The first Wisconsin Lakes Convention was held on the UW-Stevens Point campus in 1978. In conjunction with this convention, a group of lake district leaders began discussions on the formation of a statewide association of lake districts.

The year 1981 was significant for two reasons. On March 21, 1981, at the Second Bi-Annual Convention of Lake District Commissioners, the Wisconsin Association of Lake Districts (WALD) was formally created. Lowell Klessig chaired the first meeting. Pat Lane of Lake Noquebay was elected first president. That year WALD counted 35 member lake districts and a budget of $1,800. Ten years later, WALD membership had expanded to 120 lake districts, with a budget of $18,000.

Also during 1981, during a state budget crisis, cost-sharing funds in the DNR and staff resources at UWEX and DNR were eliminated. Lake districts continued to function under Chapter 33. But, the constituency of this program had grown strong enough to regard this blow as anything but temporary. In fact, the setback seemed to strengthen the partnership.

The partnership now included the Wisconsin Federation of Lakes, Wisconsin Association of Lake Districts, UWEX, UW-Stevens Point, and DNR. The partners co-sponsored the annual convention and undertook other joint efforts. The joint efforts also included lobbying to restore the staff resources for lake management and financial assistance to lake districts. Efforts of the broad based constituency paid off. The 1985 state budget began restoring the funds and tied the funding for the program to marine fuel tax collections, rather than general purpose revenues.

The Wisconsin Association of Lake Districts boasts of its legislative efforts on behalf of Wisconsin lakes. Among the key legislative actions it supported were the Drunk

LAKE STEWARDSHIP AWARD WINNERS
INDIVIDUAL
1996 Mary Bierman
1995 John Seibel
1994 John Avery
1993 Alice Clausing
1992 Mary Danoski
1991 Lloyd Christenson
1990 Jim Holperin
1989 Lisa Conley
1988 Kathy Aron
1987 Elmer Goetsch

Boating Bill of 1985; low interest loans for lake districts from the Trust Fund Loan Program; establishment of the Water Resources Account, which holds the funds transferred from the marine fuel tax collections to support staff resources and grants to local communities for lake management purposes; the creation of a Lake Management Planning Grant program; and the Environmental Education Grant Program. The association also successfully lobbied to expand Chapter 33, giving lake districts the authority to operate boat patrols, develop recreational boating facilities and, in some instances, regulate surface waters. In subsequent legislation, the partnership was able to secure marine fuel tax revenues for lake protection activities, including the purchase of environmentally sensitive areas. At the turn of the decade, WALD was a positive force on behalf of Wisconsin's inland lakes.

MERGER — STRENGTH IN NUMBERS

*I*n 1992, the Wisconsin Association of Lake Districts and the Wisconsin Federation of Lakes merged to form the Wisconsin Association of Lakes, which assumed chapter status in the North American Lake Management Society. Elmer Goetsch of Three Lakes in Oneida County, long time leader in the Wisconsin Federation of Lakes, was elected chairman of the board. Lisa Conley of Waukesha County was elected president. Other elected officers were Mary Platner as secretary, Al Habeck as treasurer and Ollie Thelander as assistant treasurer. A budget of $33,000 and a dues

---

LAKE STEWARDSHIP AWARD WINNERS

GROUP

1996 Loon Lake District

1995 Lake Ripley Management District

1994 Balsam Lake Protection and Rehabilitation District

1993 Long Lake Fishing Club

1992 City of Tomah Lake Committee/District

1991 Black Otter Lake District

1990 Bullhead Lake Advancement Association

1989 Town of Delavan Lake Committee

1988 Lake Puckaway District/Association

1987 Rollingstone Lake District

Elmer Goetsch (center) and John Avery (right) at Trees for Tomorrow in Eagle River attending the Northeast Wisconsin Lakes Convention. August 1990.

Mary Platner, Wisconsin Association of Lakes President, 1996.

LAKE STEWARDSHIP
AWARD WINNERS

PUBLIC SERVICE

1996 Steve Field

1995 Tom Wilson

1994 Harvey Stower

1993 Les Aspin

schedule were also adopted during the convention.

The Wisconsin Association of Lakes is headquartered on the UW-Stevens Point campus and has an administrative coordinator. Since its inception, this association has successfully instituted expanded volunteer efforts such as the Adopt-A-Lake program for youth.

In November, 1995 Lisa Conley of Lac La Belle in Waukesha County, became the first citizen president of the North American Lake Management Society. She would take the cooperative spirit of the Wisconsin program to the nation.

A NEW GENERATION

A strong partnership and a new, stronger association allowed Lowell Klessig to shift his energies to other endeavors. While he remains involved as senior advisor committed to the citizen protection of their "commonwealth," the Inland Lakes Program has new leadership. UW-Stevens Point/Extension specialist Robert Korth represents the University of Wisconsin. Jeffrey Bode is the lead DNR professional in the partnership. There is also new leadership on the board of the Wisconsin Association of Lakes. They are building the program and the association. They are expanding the volunteer efforts and the technical and educational programs that support the lakes.

As he turned over leadership to the new generation, Lowell Klessig observed the following: "No other state has a partnership like Wisconsin. Though widely envied it has not been replicated. To capture the unique and extended relationships among the Wisconsin Association of Lakes, the Wisconsin Department of Natural Resources, and University of Wisconsin Extension, and to describe the collection of lake management efforts by 800 citizen lake monitors, 400 lake associations, 200 lake districts, state and district DNR staff, and campus and county Extension staff, the Wisconsin Lakes Program was renamed the Wisconsin Lakes Partnership. The name has finally caught up with the spirit."

Other state level University faculty and staff who provided support in early years:

Professor Harold (Bud) Jordahl, Department of Urban and Regional Planning, UW Madison/Extension.

Mr. Robert Sterrett, UWEX Environmental Resources Center.

Mr. Ronald Hennings, Wisconsin Geological and Natural History Survey, UWEX.

Professor George Gibson, UWEX Environmental Resources Center.

Professor Al Bedrosian, UW Marinette.

Professors Stanley Nichols and James Peterson, Environmental Resources Center, UW-Madison/Extension.

Professor William Swenson, UW-Superior.

Professor Douglas Yanggen, Environmental Resources Center and Department of Agricultural Economics, UW-Madison/Extension.

Professor Robert Bright, UW-Extension.

Representative Harvey Black addressing the Wisconsin Lakes Convention. To his right, Senator C. Chvala.

Local Government and Lake Property Owners who Built the Partnership -- First Board of Directors of Wisconsin Association of Lake Districts

Pat Lane, President, Crivitz

William L. Walters, Vice-President, Shorewood

Al W. Larson, Secretary, Chilton

Norm Schein, Treasurer, Galesville

Eleanor H. Brenneke, Hortonville

Lloyd N. Christenson, Amery

James A. Daniels, St. Germain

Don Grim, Balsam Lake

Robert H. Kupper, Tomah

Ray Nereng, Blairgerald Schwarten, Burlington

George Vollert, Star Prairie

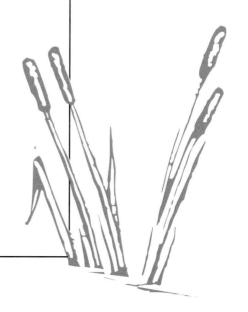

The Balsam Lodge on Spider Lake near Hayward was a traditional Wisconsin summer resort of the 1930s and '40s.

(Courtesy, State Historical Society of Wisconsin)

LODGE BALSAM LODGE ON SPIDER LAT
1IS.

CHAPTER SEVEN

PUTTING THE
WISCONSIN
TOURISM
INDUSTRY
ON THE MAP

*T*he winding path that led to the formation of the Wisconsin Tourism Federation in October 1979 began in the late 1940s. At that time much of the recreation industry, the small resort owners in particular, maintained the tradition of the north woods wilderness camp. Plumbing was primitive and furniture worn, while insect control meant hanging a fly swatter on the cabin wall. Many operators of these small, family-owned businesses had limited training in management, marketing and finance. There were, of course, exceptions, but large and well-managed facilities were not the norm.

Eagle River downtown marquee when Governor Knowles caught the 1,000th muskie in the Vilas County Muskie Marathon. These promotions meant a lot for area tourism businesses. Gene Radloff, UW-Extension is with the Governor. 1960s.

During this period, even in Northern Wisconsin, only a few local officials, resort owners and residents recognized the potential of tourism as the backbone of the local economy. The season was short. Families vacationed only in summer, while a few hardy anglers visited in spring and hunters came up in the fall. Marketing practices were behind the times. Disbursed across the northern half of the state, small businesses were not organized and thus unable to unite as an economic force.

UW-Madison's College of Agriculture was providing some educational assistance for resort and restaurant operators through its Extension Service. In response to county agent and district administrator requests, several extension campus specialists were traveling north to offer workshops. The first series of workshops offered in 1948 appropriately focused on interior furnishings, sanitation and insect control. In 1949, the list of subjects expanded to include marketing. UW-Madison professors Bryant Kearl, Claron Burnett, Lloyd Bostian and Maurice White were teaching workshops on ad writing, business letters, brochure layout and design.

LOCAL AND REGIONAL TOURISM ORGANIZATIONS -- VILAS COUNTY EXTENSION OFFICE IN THE LEAD

*I*n the late 1940s Herman Smith took over as the Vilas County Extension Agent. The landscape was slowly recovering from pioneer logging and misguided attempts to foster agriculture. Smith was convinced that the scenic beauty and abundant natural resources made the region most suitable for strong, tourist-based industry. He set out to convince local leaders that the infant touristry sector could be developed into a major economic sector which would revitalize the northern economy. Formidable barriers stood in the way.

Smith faced apathy from local industry and government leaders. He was also dealing with an Extension Service focused on agriculture, home economics and 4-H programs, which had not yet developed an understanding of the educational needs of other client groups. He was to bring about change on two fronts: education and institution building.

In a career spanning twenty years, Herman organized and taught the educational programs that helped recreation-tourism operators upgrade their skills. He teamed up with Don Schink, state specialist, and Sherman Wise, county Extension agent in Sawyer County, to offer programs on financing improvements and expansions. The UW-Madison specialists he identified in Journalism, Agricultural Economics, Home Economics, Forestry, Entomology and other departments became resource people to the tourism operators. He also organized resort tours to help resort owners learn from each other.

It was at the continual urging of Herman Smith, and the business leaders he had organized into chambers of commerce and other groups, that the University of Wisconsin decided to hire the first state specialist in recreation, Larry Monthey, on an experimental basis in 1955. There were also other

World Championship Snowmobile Derby at Eagle River in the early 1980s. Snowmobiling events opened up an important revenue source for Northwoods tourism businesses.

efforts within UW-Madison to support the recreation/tourism sector. Agricultural Economist Syd Staniforth and his colleagues were conducting studies of recreation enterprises. Isadore Fine at the School of Business was publishing tourism business reports. Richard Schuster, Gale VandeBerg and Don Schink were providing planning support to counties through the Community Development Unit.

Northwoods Council Officers. Left to right, unknown, Roy Almen, President; Herman Smith, Secretary/Treasurer.

These efforts were not organized, however, until the establishment of the Recreation Resources Center in 1969. Under the initial leadership of Harold "Bud" Jordahl and Gale VandeBerg, and with a grant from the Upper Great Lakes Regional Commission, the Resources Center focused the UW's educational efforts and would go on to support the recreation-tourism industry through research, education and leadership development for 25 years.

In addition to education, Herman Smith made a significant difference in the area of organization building. He took a region where communities, counties and businesses were competing with each other; where there was no communication among people or organizations on their common goals; where there was no sharing of ideas, resources or information; where there was no unified voice, clear leadership or a focal point for external relations, and slowly changed it all.

Herman organized resort meetings in Vilas County, which led to the formation of community groups. These community groups organized in 1959 to form the Wisconsin Head Waters Association. The purpose of this group was to cut down on costly duplication in advertising among Vilas County communities and to coordinate community events. Herman served as president and acting secretary.

In six years, the Wisconsin Head Waters Association was reorganized into the Vilas County Chamber of Commerce. Within its first two years of operation, 1955-1957, the Vilas County Chamber acquired the membership of 15 local chambers and came to represent more than 1,000 individuals. Herman Smith remained as secretary and moving force of the Chamber for ten years. Eugene Radloff, Vilas County Extension Resource Development Agent, followed Herman in the secretary role for the Vilas County Chamber for another 24 years.

While the Vilas County Chamber of Commerce had become a positive force in policy development, Herman Smith recognized the need for a broader base of representation. He laid the groundwork for a two-county chamber of commerce, covering Vilas and Oneida counties. Other counties in the region, impressed with the effectiveness of the Vilas County setup, requested membership in the regional chamber. The result was an eight-county organization that incorporated in 1963 as the Northwoods Council. The major goals of the Northwoods Council were to promote and advertise the businesses of the area, ensure communications among organizations in the region, provide legislative input with a unified voice, and to support and develop educational programs for members. Herman served as secretary and driving force behind this organization until his retirement.

Finally, Herman Smith went the last step. He was among the founders of Hospitality Industry, Inc., a statewide coalition of tourism organizations. The Northwoods Council became a charter member of this statewide group.

The Northwoods Council provided a strong voice for the interests and needs of the region which had formerly gone unnoticed.

Don Schink (right) presenting the Northern Great Lakes Development Committee Report to Governor Knowles, 1966.

It is also recognized as one of the pioneers (along with Indianhead Country) of regional tourism organizations. It is a credit to the leadership of the Northwoods Council that, in the confusion following new administrative rules and reorganization of the state tourism function in the 1970s, they were the only group which could file an acceptable marketing plan for state cooperative funding during 1977. While many relatively wealthier regions of the state had difficulty raising the funds to cost-share state promotional dollars, the Northwoods Council was consistently able to raise the funds to take full advantage of state promotional funds.

Herman Smith's lasting contribution was in helping change the attitudes of local citizens. He helped them become more coordinated and more communicative by demonstrating the effectiveness of working together. He also instilled the value of being a catalyst in a new generation of Extension specialists, including this author. He always said, "Remember, we work for the little people." Thus, he also influenced the value system of a generation of University professionals who felt honored just by serving the "little people."

Upper Great Lakes Regional Commission tourism project state leaders--left to right, John Hodge, Michigan State University, Paul Stelmanchek, University of Minnesota, Don Schink, University of Wisconsin.

THE TOURISM INDUSTRY ORGANIZING AT THE STATE LEVEL

In April 1969, Donald Schink, Community Resource Development Specialist with UW-Extension, presented tourism industry leaders with a paper titled "Suggested Organization -- Wisconsin Hospitality Industry, Inc." Industry leaders had been mulling over the need for a statewide organization to mirror the changes within state government.

A new and strengthened Recreation and Tourism Unit had been organized in the Wisconsin Department of Natural Resources. Tourism industry leaders were working to create a Recreation-Tourism committee in the State Legislature. Also proposed was a Recreation-Tourism Center at the University of Wisconsin. Resident instruction programs were being developed at the Wisconsin State University-Stout and other state institutions of higher education.

Some industry leaders such as Jack Gray of the Wisconsin Dells and Ted Campbell of the Wisconsin Motel Association were working closely with Don Schink to organize the hospitality industry associations. They felt a strong need to bring together state associations and local and regional tourism groups to communicate with each other, to collaborate in expanding the tourism business and to speak with one voice on important issues.

They decided to invite leaders of hospitality and tourism organizations to a joint meeting. Jack Gray, a prominent industry leader and President of the Wisconsin Dells Chamber of Commerce at the time, issued the letter of invitation. Don Schink was assigned the task of developing a "white paper" regarding an umbrella organization. At this historic meeting in Madison, the leaders of Wisconsin's recreation-tourism industry decided to form an umbrella organization, tentatively titled Hospitality Unlimited, and to hold a joint convention of all associations in October 1969, in Madison.

Don Schink laid out the purposes of the proposed organization as follows:

1. Permit direct representation of the major sectors of the tourism business and each organized area association.

2. Support a full-time staff.

3. Be a first line discussion and decision group for recommending matters of priority for consideration by the Wisconsin Tourism Council, Division of Tourism, University of Wisconsin and other organizations and agencies.

4. Wield powerful influence on the legislature in accomplishing needed legislative changes.

5. Weld together both large and small segments of Wisconsin businesses that have a stake in the tourist and recreation business.

The partners: Jack Gray, Executive Director of Wisconsin Dells Chamber of Commerce and Don Schink, UW-Extension, 1969.

After extensive discussion among leaders of the industry associations, Hospitality Industry, Inc. was registered in August of 1969 by Theodore Campbell of the Wisconsin Motel Association. The purpose of the organization was spelled out in Article 3 of the Articles of Incorporation, which read, "to perform any and all acts necessary to develop, promote and further the recreational industries and facilities located within the State of Wisconsin by such means as the corporation shall from time to time deem appropriate and such other activities permissible under the Chapter 181 of the Wisconsin Statutes."

The original members of the corporation were the Wisconsin Campground Owners, Wisconsin Innkeepers Association, Wisconsin Motel

UW-Extension agents involved in tourism and recreation at a planning meeting with the DNR's Ray Mueller, back row left.

Association, Wisconsin Recreation Industries, Inc. and the Wisconsin Restaurant Association.

The five major industry associations brought with them a membership of 2,550. Additionally, the area groups joined Hospitality Industry, Inc. with their 1,328 members. The area associations and their representatives were as follows:

Green Bay Visitors and Travel Bureau, William Brault
Milwaukee Convention Bureau, Fred Daiger
Yellow Thunder Association/Wisconsin Dells Area, Chauncey Gannon
Southern Wisconsin Vacationland Association, Zip Coon
Blackhawk Land Association-Prairie Du Chien Area, Barney Holland
Great Rivers Country-La Crosse Area, Morris Olson
Northwoods Council, Herman Smith

The leadership of the new organization was thinking big for its first convention. They were preparing for an attendance of 1,000. Only a few hundred showed up. But, it was a start. Subsequent conventions would build on the initial number. In the mid-1970s, the Hospitality Industry, Inc. convention would become the Governor's Conference on Tourism, with thousands attending in the 1990s.

As the tourism industry was getting organized, leaders of the resort segment of the industry were pressuring UW administrators to provide the same type of research and education support they so ably delivered to the agricultural sector for the recreation-tourism businesses, as well. Jerry Loar, owner of Dillman's Sand Lake Lodge and President of Wisconsin Recreation Industries, Inc., was leading the charge. Mainly as a consequence of this pressure and with a $45,000 grant from the Upper Great Lakes Regional

COUNTY EXTENSION AGENTS WITH SIGNIFICANT CONTRIBUTIONS TO REGIONAL TOURISM ORGANIZATIONS IN THE 1970S

Everett Olsen
Iowa County

Herbert Kinney
Iron County

Irvin Leverenz
Lincoln County

Richard Williams
La Crosse County

Eugene Radloff
Vilas County

Norm Rabl
Jefferson County

INITIAL DIRECTORS OF HOSPITALITY INDUSTRY, INC.

Theodore W. Campbell, Treasurer
Campbell's Motel, Janesville (Representing the Motel Association)

John Bjork
Skogmo Cafe, Chippewa Falls (Representing Wisconsin Restaurant Association)

Eugene Carmin
Sandman Inn, Wisconsin Dells (Representing the Motel Association)

Jerry Loar
Dillman's Sand Lake Lodge, Lac du Flambeau (Representing Wisconsin Recreation Industries)

Art Huebner
Park Falls (Representing Wisconsin Recreation Industries)

Ed Doyle
Doyle Hotels and Motels, Rice Lake   (Representing Wisconsin Innkeepers)

Chauncey Gannon
Gannon's Birchwood Resort, Lodi (Representing Wisconsin Campground Association)

Carl Weber, President
Waukesha (Representing Wisconsin Innkeepers)

Milton Schmidt
Camp Rubidell, Watertown (Representing Wisconsin Campground Association)

Elmer Conforti
Milwaukee (Representing Wisconsin Restaurant Association)

Donald Fisher
Valhalla Don-Ess Family Camping Resort, Glenbeulah (Representing Wisconsin Campground Association)

Richard Murray (SBA) left, Kolby Schrichte of the Wisconsin Restaurant Association, center, and Gale VandeBerg, UW-Extension at an educational meeting on business finance at UW-Stevens Point.

Commission, the Recreation Resources Center was established in UW-Extension in 1969. Internal reallocation of funds by a series of deans (Gale VandeBerg, Glen Pulver and Robert Rieck) to this Center helped it provide significant support in research, education and leadership development to the growing recreation-tourism sector.

Don Schink continued his support of the fledgling Hospitality Industries, Inc. It was a truly volunteer run organization. It had no staff. Don Schink and his UW office, first in the College of Agriculture at UW-Madison, then in UW-Extension provided the support. Schink organized the Board of Directors meetings, chaired the sessions if the president was absent, took the minutes and carried the required communication among the directors and the membership. He also helped the Board organize the annual conventions, assisting with the development of the program and securing speakers in partnership with various Board members.

Don Schink also instilled in the staff of the newly formed Recreation Resources Center the importance of building leadership in the industry through support of the volunteer leaders. The Recreation Resources Center excelled in this regard in the 1970s and '80s. Numerous industry organizations would receive support from Sue Sadowske, Rollie Cooper, Jack Gray, Walter Tetzlaff, Milton Strauss and Ayse Somersan, as well as Don Schink. Among the organizations receiving such support were Wisconsin Association of Campground Operators, Wisconsin Recreation Industries, Inc., regional tourism organizations, Wisconsin Bed and Breakfast Association, as well as the Hospitality Industry, Inc. and the Wisconsin Tourism Federation.

Hospitality Industries, Inc. served the important purposes of communication and coordination within the recreation-tourism industry. But, the industry still did not have political clout. Numerous pleas for expansion of state promotional funds and support were falling on deaf ears. In 1979, during the presidency of Joseph Waters of Wisconsin Association of Campground Operators, Hospitality Industries, Inc. changed its name to the Wisconsin Tourism Federation. The new organization expanded its membership and retained a lobbyist. Tourism organizations would now start speaking with one voice within the decision-making circles.

The election of Tommy Thompson as Wisconsin Governor in 1986 truly changed the political influence of the Wisconsin Tourism Federation. Governor Thompson's first term brought major increases in state promotional funds. The long awaited dream of the recreation-tourism sector, to have its own state department, became a reality during Governor Thompson's second term. Ironically, the shuffling of positions in creating the new Department of Tourism in 1995 reduced the Recreation Resources Center to below critical mass. UW-Extension closed the Center in 1996.

The Wisconsin Tourism Industry was now on the map. It was recognized as a major economic force within the state.

The Kickapoo in flood at Ontario, 1959.
Flood control was one of the initial reasons
for damming the Kickapoo.

(Courtesy, State Historical Society

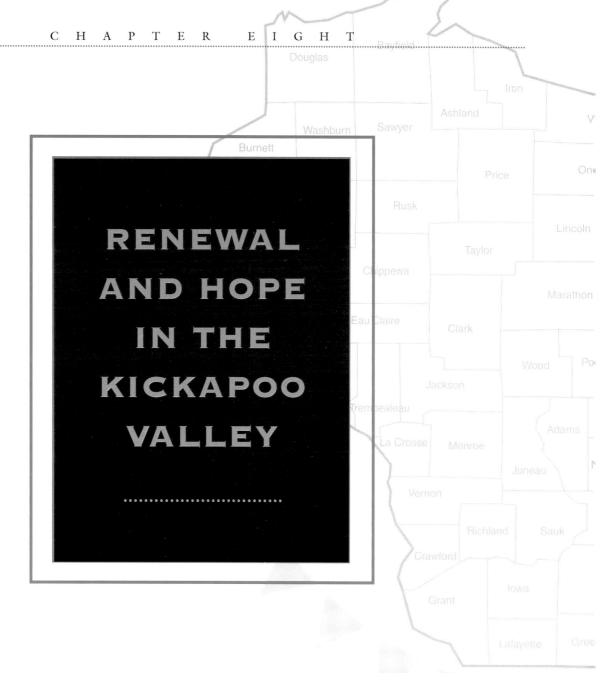

RENEWAL AND HOPE IN THE KICKAPOO VALLEY

*I*n the August, 1994 issue of *Silent Sports Magazine*, Eric Wuennenberg character-
ized the story of the Kickapoo River Valley as one of "Rejection, Redemption and
Renewal". It was a good summary of the decades long struggle over the fate of one of
southwestern Wisconsin's most valuable resources.

The battle between the advocates of a flood control and reservoir project and environ-
mentalists who questioned destroying one of the state's most scenic canoeing sites came
to a resolution with the creation of The Kickapoo Valley State Reserve, a vast natural area
which includes 454 archeological sites, trails, boat landings, campgrounds and an educational center. Most important, a citizen's body, with most of its members from the Valley,
will set the land management policy for the property.

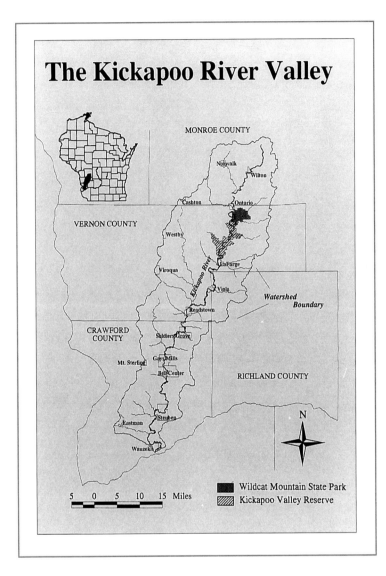

The Kickapoo River Valley

MONROE COUNTY

Norwalk

Wilton

Cashton   Ontario

VERNON COUNTY

Westby

Viroqua   LaFarge

Viola

Watershed
Boundary

Readstown

CRAWFORD
COUNTY   Soldiers Grove

Gays Mills

Mt. Sterling

Bell Center

RICHLAND COUNTY

Steuben

Eastman

N

Wauzeka

5   0   5   10   15   Miles

■ Wildcat Mountain State Park
▨ Kickapoo Valley Reserve

A map of the Kickapoo
River Watershed; State and
Federal owned land
highlighted.

With this action, citizens of the Valley have reclaimed their control over the future of their communities and have put the grieving process of two decades to an end.

Among the major actors in the renewal process were state and local officials taking initiatives to begin a healing process, local residents participating in a grass-roots visioning and planning exercise, University of Wisconsin contributing staff for planning and research, state and federal legislators responding with authorizing and funding legislation. The redemption and renewal process also included Alan Anderson, UW-Extension professor of Community Resource Development, who helped the citizens of the Kickapoo Valley take the lead in shaping their future.

The Kickapoo Valley is approximately 500,000 acres over 70 miles north and south. The Valley has 16 incorporated communities. The two cities are Viroqua and Westby, with populations of 4,000 and 1,400, respectively. The historic economic base of the region is agriculture, with relatively small farms. The per capita income of the area in 1990 was $6,700, while the state averaged $12,300. Also, the Valley has been prone to flash flooding. The area has been flooded at least ten times since the turn of the 20th Century, with two of these classified as "100 year" floods in 1907 and 1978.

Flood control efforts for the Kickapoo Valley date back to the 1930s. But, the real action started in 1962 with Congress authorizing a flood control dam and a lake at La Farge. The plans were finalized in the mid-1960s, with flood control and economic development through recreation and tourism the main goals of the La Farge Dam Project. Property acquisition at fair market value started in 1969 and, eventually, 140 farms were purchased from their reluctant owners.

With the La Farge dam half complete in 1975, a reevaluation of the cost-benefit ratio found the dam uneconomical and brought the project to a halt. So began a twenty year period of bitter debate on the La Farge dam throughout the Valley. The people who invested in land, hoping to cash in on the tourism boom, demanded that the dam be finished. Most of the 140 farmers who were forced to sell their land wanted it back. Everyone was disgusted with a government that spent $18 million of tax dollars and left behind an unfinished dam surrounded by hostile people.

The local outrage was fueled by the devastating effect of losing 140 farms, a third of the students in the school system and, possibly, a fourth of the economic base of the La Farge business district. Not only were the dreams of economic growth through tourism shattered,

The earthen dam constructed in the early 1970s which would have provided flood control and a lake for recreational development. Construction was stopped for environmental and financial reasons and precipitated a 20-year controversy. (Photo: Wolfgang Hoffman, CALS)

but the region was severely harmed by the loss of working farms. The ensuing years brought further division into the community over what to do with the property. With no consensus on future direction the unifying force was distrust and hatred for government.

In 1991, Governor Tommy Thompson, with strong appeals from Senator Brian Rude and Representative DuWayne Johnsrud, asked President Buzz Shaw of the University of Wisconsin for assistance to help the region plan its economic future. A three year initiative was designed by President Shaw and Chancellor Patrick G. Boyle of UW-Extension to place an economic development agent in the Valley to assist the region in its attempts to improve its economic base. The School of Natural Resources at the College of Agriculture and Life Sciences joined the partnership to provide research and staff support.

Professor Alan Anderson of UW-Extension was introduced by Governor Thompson at a meeting at La Farge High School in August, 1991. Most residents were skeptical about this meager response from their government after 16 years of failed lawsuits and bitter debate. But, the time was right and Al Anderson was the right person to help Valley residents start the redemption process. The citizen participation model put in place in the Kickapoo Valley will long be studied as an approach that works in land use and economic development planning.

STEPS IN ENGAGING THE CITIZENRY

*D*ouglas Bradley started a 1994 article in UW System's Wisconsin Ideas titled *Lighting a Flame in the Kickapoo Valley* with a quote from Socrates: "Education is not the filling of a vessel but the kindling of a flame."

A typical Valley farm. Farms tend to be smaller than the state average, with small percentage of tillable land. (Photo: Wolfgang Hoffman, CALS)

The kindling of a flame is what local residents needed to start the process to take back 8,500 acres of the Valley. Alan Anderson did not realize when he accepted the position in the Valley that he was going to kindle that flame.

Looking back at his work in the Kickapoo Valley Alan Anderson says, "I knew the local residents were still angry about the dam issue, but I thought I would be asked to come up with other efforts to help revitalize the area. I was wrong." Anderson summarizes the steps in the consensus building process as follows:

◆ Formed a citizens participation committee, with representatives of each village and city appointed to this advisory body, as well as representatives of the financial, business and tourism communities. County board members and elected area representatives to the Wisconsin Legislature also joined the advisory committee.

◆ This group met six times and learned about the economy of the Valley and the changes in the broader economic picture affecting their possible futures.

◆ When asked to set priorities for what should happen in the future, the group decided that creating jobs was their first priority and the second priority was to resolve the long-standing dispute over the La Farge dam.

◆ In lengthy discussions, advisory committee members decided that job creation was a local community issue and needed to be tackled at that level. The Valley-wide issue they would tackle was the dam and the tourism potential of the Valley.

◆ Under early leadership from Dr. Robert Horwich, an expert on community based nature preserves and sanctuaries, an initial proposal was prepared for the use of the property. A drafting committee of the advisory board then started reworking Dr. Horwich's proposal with additional alternative approaches to the control of the property and its management.

◆ In the spring of 1993 the Drafting Committee of the Kickapoo Valley Advisory Committee released its plan for public review. The plan, titled *Proposal for the Kickapoo Community Reserve and Center for Rural Sustainability,* called for the creation of a special state authority to assume control of the La Farge dam property from the US Corps of Engineers, as well as management through a committee appointed by the Governor.

◆ In the months following the release of the draft plan, numerous public meetings and formal approvals by local units of government underscored unprecedented support for the concepts by Valley residents. The people of the Kickapoo Valley had decided to keep the land public, carefully develop its ecotourism potential and maintain a strong hand in its future management. The plan also received the support of state agencies and environmental groups. It was now time for legislative action.

One of the many trout streams in the Valley. Projects are working to improve water quality and the trout fishery in the watershed. (Photo: Wolfgang Hoffman, CALS)

STEPS IN THE LEGISLATIVE PROCESS

Senate Bill 721, authorizing the creation of a Kickapoo Valley Reserve Board, passed the Wisconsin State Senate by a vote of 29-3 in

Example of dialogue going on between state and federal government representatives. Left to right: Senator Brian Rude, Congressman Steve Gunderson, LaVerne Ausman, head of district office for Gunderson. 1966. (Photo: Epitaph News)

March, 1994. The bill passed the Wisconsin State Assembly by unanimous vote the day after Senate approval. Senator Brian Rude and Representative DuWayne Johnsrud convinced their colleagues in both houses of the state Legislature that setting in place the framework for the management of the land was essential in the process to convince the US Congress to deauthorize the La Farge Dam Project and turn the land over to the state. They went into the state legislative process with a very strong hand based on the strong consensus of the people of the Kickapoo Valley behind their efforts.

The flame lighted in the Kickapoo Valley in 1991 continued to burn as Governor Tommy Thompson signed the bill into law in April 1994.

WISCONSIN CONGRESSIONAL DELEGATION DELIVERS

*T*he efforts to transfer the La Farge Dam Project to the state failed when the US Senate failed to take action on the Water Resources and Development Act in the fall of 1994. The measure was introduced in the

A meeting at the State Capitol to review progress toward state and federal legislation. Left to right: Alan Anderson (UW-Extension), Lou Kowalski (US Corps of Engineers), aide to Senator B. Rude, Senator Brian Rude, Representative from State Legislative Council, Representative DuWayne Johnsrud, Rebecca Zahm (currently on Reserve Management Board). 1993. (Photo: From Epitaph News, taken by Ron Johnson)

House of Representatives by Steve Gunderson and Tom Petri as a part of this omnibus federal water bill. Senators Russ Feingold and Herb Kohl introduced the measure in the US Senate. Funding for the transfer, as well as funding for the completion of highway 131 from Rockton to Ontario and development of the area for tourism, was also temporarily stalled when this water quality legislation did not get to a vote.

This eleventh hour failure at the federal level meant waiting another twenty four months before deauthorization, transfer to the state and the allocation of $17 million in federal funds to develop the land would get another hearing. At this point the flame flickered, but no one doubted that it would survive this setback.

Alan Anderson continued his communication with Valley residents during these frustrating months. He relayed information on the reasons for the delay from the Congressional offices involved. He urged residents and local officials to start working on setting up the Reserve Board, working on mission, by-laws, job descriptions and other preparatory work to hiring a state-funded executive director. There was a lot to be done and this was a delay of great inconvenience. But, no one even thought of giving up.

Signing of the state legislation which set in place the framework for management of the land (April 1994). Left to right: Senator Rude, Representative Johnsrud, Rob Horwitz (member of Drafting Committee), Don Coleman (Town of Stark Chairman and current Board member), Jack Robinson (Vernon Co. Board and current Management Board member), George Meyer, Secretary of DNR.(Photo: Vernon County Broadcaster)

On the first day of the 104th Congress, January 3, 1995, the same bill was reintroduced in the House of Representative by Representative Steve Gunderson. The bill passed a day before the end of the session in 1996. The credit for this effort goes to representatives Gunderson and Petri, and Senators Feingold and Kohl. Representative Gunderson and Senator Feingold are credited with leading the debate in their respective houses of Congress.

Negotiations continue between US Corps of Engineers, the State Historical Society and the Ho Chunk Nation. 1996. (Photo: Epitaph News)

The Federal legislation has unique features. It responds to local requests for the Federal government to deliver on its promises of economic development. It responds to the $11 million request to pay for completing the construction of Highway 131. While the local request of $6 million for developing the tourism infrastructure of the region is overlooked, the legislation allocates $6 million for environmental cleanup of the area.

The Federal legislation also offers an option for resolving the conflict between Native American and other Kickapoo residents demands. The Ho Chunk Nation had asked that the total land be turned over to the tribe because it contained sacred sites. The Federal legislation indicates that the Ho Chunks can own 1,200 acres of land, provided they negotiate with the State of Wisconsin on how it will be co-managed with the rest of the property. The request by the Ho Chunk nation to have a voting member on the Kickapoo Reserve Governing Board will require changes in the state legislation.

THE LAND, THE INSTITUTION, THE FUTURE

*I*n 1997 the Kickapoo Reserve Management Board has hired an Executive Director and office assistant, and established an office in LaFarge. Ron Johnson is the President of the Management Board.

The immediate hurdles facing the Board and the Executive Director relate to the deadline of October 31, 1997 set by the federal legislation. By this date, the legislation requires for the State and Ho Chunk Nation to write and approve a Memorandum of Understanding that designates the 1,200 acres to be put in trust with the Bureau of Indian Affairs on behalf of the Ho Chunk Nation. It also requires a management plan for the 8,600 acres and an indication of how significant archeological sites will be protected.

Another major hurdle relates to funding. Although Congress has authorized $17 million in 1996, there has been no appropriation of additional funds for this project. Each year, the Wisconsin Congressional Delegation and interest groups will need to work with the Corps of Engineers and the full Congress to appropriate funds.

In the meantime, the Kickapoo Reserve Management Board has its focus on the future. The plans are to incorporate low-impact tourism into the project and develop a rural education/visitors center that includes a classroom. The Board intends to involve education in everything from trail development and mapping to building foot bridges, photography and drawing classes, and on-site wildlife, forestry and farm management.

The "Application Office" for Extension programs at Milwaukee, 1925. While perceived as having a rural focus, Extension has long included programs for urbanites.

(Courtesy, State Historical Society of Wisconsin)

BUILDING A RESOURCEFUL URBAN NEIGHBORHOOD

· ·

*T*he Harambee neighborhood, with a population of about 30,000 people, covers a 170 block area in the northern section of Milwaukee's central city. "Harambee" is a Swahili word that means "Let's Pull Together." In the early 1960s, there was a clear need to pull together local residents and other persons who had access to resources to improve the quality of life for Harambee residents and to make them active participants in determining their community's future.

The Reuben Harpole Family--son John, daughter Annette, wife Mildred, also a life-long Harambee resident, community activist and chair of the Harambee Health Task Force in the 1970s and 1980s.

Former Milwaukee Mayor Frank Zeidler, chair of the 13th Ward Community Council (now, Northcentral Community Council), asked Reuben Harpole, a Harambee resident and community activist, to approach UW-Milwaukee and UW-Extension for community development assistance. Thus began a relationship between a young political scientist, Dr. Belden Paulson of UW-Extension and UW-Milwaukee and Reuben Harpole, who would continue their association for over three decades.

Reuben Harpole was the advertising director of the black newspaper, *The Milwaukee Star.* He had excellent contacts in the community. Harpole and Paulson decided to spend some time listening to the Harambee residents to get a sense of what they identified as core problems. This informal listening activity alerted them to many problems. They decided to move ahead with a formal survey to identify needs with more precision.

Paulson and Harpole organized a 60-block survey in 1965. Professor Jonathan Schlesinger helped design the survey. Harpole and Paulson recruited community volunteers and worked with Schlesinger to train them to administer the survey. Agnes Cobbs was one of those volunteers. The survey findings clearly identified that educational issues and, more specifically, reading proficiency and parent-school relationships, were critical community problems. It was time for action.

Belden Paulson and Reuben Harpole started to organize tutorial centers in the community, mostly in church basements. At the height of this activity, they had 20 tutorial centers in operation. They asked Dr. A. Schoeller, head of the Reading Department in the UW-Milwaukee School of Education, to develop the curriculum and train the volunteers who would teach in the tutorial centers. The project was off the ground.

Agnes Cobbs was the coordinator of one of the best tutorial centers, located in the Mount Moriah Baptist Church. The work of the entire group was coordinated out of the Civic Center offices of Dr. Paulson's Center for Urban Community Development(CUCD). The University was getting engaged with the community.

The Central City Teacher Project evolved out of the tutorial centers. Involving key leaders on the School Board, Paulson and Harpole successfully obtained a one million dollar federal grant. The goal of this project was to develop relationships between schools and parents. At one point, they had 25 percent of the Central City schools participating in developing direct contact between the principals and teachers and the parents and students. The contact took the form of teachers' aides, who were parents and volunteers. Some of the community people involved were later in the vanguard of developing the teachers' aide program of the public schools.

These activities laid the foundation for what was to come. University professors had left their offices, listened to the people in the community, and had joined them in finding resources and solutions to their pressing problems. Also, they didn't leave when grant monies ran out. They were there for the long haul, which is what community development is all about.

There were also changes on campus. As chair of the Center for Urban Development, Belden Paulson's conviction that the Harambee community efforts were central to the University's mission facilitated the whole department's participation in various ways in the Harambee projects. Also at this time, Reuben Harpole joined the unit, first as a volunteer and, later, funded through foundation funds and, finally, through regular University appropriations. He was one of the early regular UW-Milwaukee staff drawn from the African American community.

In the meantime, the Harambee community was faced with a new challenge. The Catholic Archdiocese of Milwaukee informed the community that funds would be cut off to support their Catholic school. The residents were now faced with the challenge of converting their parochial school to a community school. Rising to the occasion, the joint

Agnes Cobbs out in the community with block leaders--Agnes, bottom right. Others--Lula Keyes, Betty Hubbard, Hazel Cook, Cora Sprewell, Huey Glass, Sherry, Mrs. Thomas.

efforts of the clergy, parents and some community minded people who lived in the St. Elizabeth Parish area resulted in the founding of the Harambee Community School in 1969. The Archdiocese provided three years of funding support in the transition.

But, the money was merely a stop-gap until other funds could be secured. In 1970, the Harambee School Board asked UW-Extension for technical assistance in helping to locate alternative financial sources and to utilize the school as a catalyst to improve the surrounding neighborhood. In response, Belden Paulson, Reuben Harpole and the CUCD staff teamed up to develop a proposal which became the Harambee Revitalization Project, with initial funding provided by Title 1 of the Higher Education Act of 1965, beginning in Spring, 1971.

The Harambee Revitalization Project focused on building a working partnership between the Harambee community itself and the resources of the larger community. Community residents worked with university faculty, staff and students in community problem solving activities. The goal was to keep as much control as possible in the hands of the community residents, while at the same time mobilizing the talents and resources of the University to assist in this ambitious effort.

The project had a slow and often troublesome developmental phase. The university and the community were breaking new ground in seeking a strategy for comprehensive community development in a poor city area. Eventually, the hard work of the early years crystallized into a number of programs and organizations which, taken together, represented a coordinated attack on neighborhood problems. The organizations which emerged from this effort in the 1970s would lay the foundation for increased support for the neighborhood in the 1980s and the 1990s.

The Harambee Revitalization Project was pathbreaking for several reasons. It was based on a sophisticated conceptual model of comprehensive community development. It built on the relationships and trust established in earlier community-university partnerships. The grant funds did not stay on campus but were mostly invested in the community volunteers who became part of the staff in the projects. This approach further expanded the leadership and professional skills of community residents. Finally, the Project attacked problems on many fronts to move towards comprehensive community development.

Harambee Kids on the steps waiting for Mrs. Ethel Mc Grew, Block Leader.

In the mid-1970s there were four major components in the Harambee Project: The Harambee Ombudsman Project, the Harambee Development Corporation and Home Improvement Project, the Harambee Health Project and the Harambee Human Services Project. Over the years, the Ombudsman Project and the Health Project have prevailed as lasting community institutions.

THE HARAMBEE OMBUDSMAN PROJECT, INC.

*T*he Harambee Ombudsman Project evolved from a series of community courses organized and taught by professor Belden Paulson through the UW-Milwaukee Political Science Department. The courses were aimed at introducing the Harambee residents to the workings of the political system and help them understand how to become active participants to bring about change. Area residents were recruited for these courses which were team-taught with elected local government representatives. In one course, area alderman and chair of the Common Council Ben Johnson was invited to act as a co-professor. County Board Supervisor Emil Stanislawski co-taught another course with Professor Paulson. This was, indeed, a real-world simulation of the workings of the political system.

Agnes Cobbs was a student in the classes, as well as a community development specialist with UW-Extension since 1967, hired by Dr. Paulson with department funds. She helped recruit the community residents for the classes. In one of the courses, as she and others were completing their assignment to identify problems on various blocks in the community and relate them to the workings of the political system, it became apparent to them that residents were having great difficulty stating their problems in concrete and specific ways that could be processed politically. They needed to translate complaints such as "there is too much crime and infestation of rats on our block" to "the shrubbery on the vacant

Reuben Harpole reading to the children at 38th Street School, March 1992.

lot at First and Hadley Streets needs to be cut so that neighborhood children can't hide in them and sanitary conditions can be improved". Once they clearly restated the problem, Alderman Ben Johnson could take their complaints to the appropriate city agencies and got immediate results. The connection was obvious.

The class proceeded to design a neighborhood ombudsman project which included the following key elements: 1) block leaders were identified and trained; 2) residents were contacted to find out the perceived community problems; 3) their problem statements were translated into agency language and submitted to the alderman's and county supervisors' offices.

Agnes Cobbs charged ahead to implement the ombudsman project, with important assistance from Todd Honeyager, a pre-law graduate of UW-Milwaukee, and several neighborhood leaders all funded by CUCD with CETA funds. She created 370 block leaders in the 170 block area. Their function was to know everything and provide leadership in their block. These block leaders organized the residents and, with the support of the City Department of Public Works, cleaned all the alleys. Legendary block leaders like Mrs. McGrew, now 95, and Mrs. Jesse Jones would get people out of bed if they saw work that needed to be done.

In the late 1970s, Agnes Cobbs, director of the Ombudsman Project, Inc., utilized her experiences to teach grass roots community organizing as a specialist with UW-Extension. Many organizations, including the public utilities, attended her classes. She continues in retirement to offer workshops to assist residents with their personal finances, as well on ways to better their community.

Reuben Harpole, who can be considered a co-founder of CUCD, has worked with UW-Extension and UW-Milwaukee as an Urban Outreach Specialist since 1966. He continues to bring his special talent, that of a connector of communities with resources, to many aspects of life in Milwaukee and has won numerous awards for his leadership.

HARAMBEE HEALTH TASK FORCE MEMBERSHIP, 1976
TASK FORCE OFFICERS

Mildred Harpole, Chair
Director, Fair Housing & Equal Opportunities Office, HUD

Constantine Panagis, M.D., Vice-Chair
Commissioner of Health, City of Milwaukee

Jane Schultz, Secretary
Associate Director of Public Relations, Medical College of Wisconsin

COMMUNITY REPRESENTATIVES

Geneva McGee, Former Director, Peoples Free Health Clinic

June Perry, Director, New Concept Self-Development Center

Reuben Harpole, Specialist, Center for Urban Community Development, UW-Extension

Todd Honeyager, Harambee Ombudsman Project

Marcia Coggs, State Assemblywoman

Sister Mary Lou Slowey, R.N., Harambee Community School

Iola Lockhart, R.N., Family Hospital

Barbara Whitmore, R.N., Public Health Nurse Consultant

Frederich Birts, Madison Area Technical College

INSTITUTIONAL REPRESENTATIVES

Donovan W. Riley, Medical College of Wisconsin

Fred Matthies, M.D., Milwaukee County Medical Complex

Elizabeth Regan, Professor, UW-Extension

Belden Paulson, Professor, Center for Urban Community Development, UW-Extension

Fred Blodgett, M.D., Milwaukee Children's Hospital

Janet Harvey, R.N., Family Practice Clinic, St. Mary's Hospital

The Harambee Ombudsman Project, Inc. has operated as a community-based non-profit organization since the early 1970s. It incorporated in 1979. It has an 11-member board of directors, with a 73% Harambee community resident participation rate on the board. Sherman Hill, current director, proudly summarizes the continuing contributions of the Ombudsman Project. This organization serves the central city by offering education, counseling, alcohol and drug abuse treatment, prevention and referrals, neighborhood improvement services, foster care placement, licensing and supervision, home buying counseling and community organizing. It has grown into a neighborhood planning, leadership and community development organization.

Belden Paulson and his colleagues have made a lasting contribution to a central city community through the long-term investment of their time and talent, as well as through their innovative approach to neighborhood revitalization and university-community partnership.

Agnes Cobbs training volunteers.

THE HARAMBEE HEALTH PROJECT

*P*rofessors Belden Paulson and Daniel Folkman, in their case study of the Harambee Revitalization Project, describe the precipitating event for the Harambee Health Project as a television program on the status of health in Milwaukee's black community. They note that "this program initiated a series of discussions between the UW-Extension staff and the State Department of Health and Social Services concerning a proposed mother-infancy program for Milwaukee."

At the same time, Sister Mary Lou Slowey, the nurse at the Harambee Community School, contacted UW-Extension about her concern for the health of the families of children attending school. These contacts led to a series of meetings convened by Reuben Harpole, community development specialist with UW-Extension. Discussion centered on the status of care in Harambee, with representatives from the Harambee Community School, UW-Extension, the County Medical Complex, Health and Social Services, and several persons from various medical and health institutions in the Milwaukee area.

Sister Mary Lou Slowey's alert and the early meetings later developed into the Harambee Health Committee. The Health Committee, through its work in 1975 and early 1976, developed a comprehensive family health history model to be used in maintaining a health record of Harambee residents. Later, the Committee developed a proposal on a neighborhood health center and requested medical backup from a local hospital.

In early 1976, the Medical College of Wisconsin, under the leadership of its president David Carley, contacted UW-Extension staff and Harambee residents to explore the development of a community-based health outreach program. The meetings also included the City Health Department and the County Medical Complex representatives. Agreement was reached to work together to plan a comprehensive, coordinated health delivery and preventive care system in the Harambee community. The expertise of the participating institutions would be combined with the involvement of residents through the Harambee Health Committee and the Harambee Ombudsman Project. With the counsel and assistance of Barbara Whitmore, a proposal was developed to seek public and private funding. Also at this time, the city of Milwaukee assigned a health outreach worker to the Harambee Ombudsman to help define the role and responsibilities of health outreach workers operating through the neighborhood health center.

Dr. Belden Paulson and Agnes Cobbs at Ms. Cobbs' retirement. March 1992.

By 1976, the Harambee Health Committee had evolved into the Harambee Health Task Force, with membership from the community, state and local government, the medical community and the university. The Task Force developed a proposal to seek funding to carry out the following objectives: 1) assess the health needs of the community; 2) evaluate the health delivery system in terms of accessibility, responsiveness, effectiveness, and degree of coordination with the community; 3) develop a pilot system for health screening, referrals, primary care services, community health education and health outreach, in close cooperation with the Ombudsman Project; 4) develop a long range plan for governance and funding based on the first year experience of the program.

The proposal was ready in June 1977, but was turned down by the

McBeath Foundation. Other sources, including the Milwaukee Foundation, also were dead ends. When the prospects looked bleak, the Medical College of Wisconsin gave a $28,000 grant to help establish a Harambee Neighborhood Health Resource Center. This was a great victory, albeit far short of the funding needed to operate a community health center. But, support would keep coming to keep the dream alive. Milwaukee County agreed to provide two rooms in the Garfield Park Pavilion. The Downtown Medical and Health Services assured the Center of physician backup as needed.

Just as the Harambee Health Resource Center was about to get started, funds became available from the Robert Wood Johnson Foundation (RWJ) to fund a Milwaukee City and County coalition proposal to establish health care centers in Milwaukee neighborhoods. There was now $3 million on the table. The Harambee Health Task Force, under the leadership of Mildred Harpole, negotiated with city and county authorities to have one of the health centers located in the Harambee neighborhood. The proposal was accepted in June, 1978.

The health Task Force now faced a major decision -- should it continue its efforts to maintain the Health Resource Center or should it meld its resources into the proposed RWJ Center, which would provide a broader array of health services, as well as bring jobs and income to the community. Task Force members, after lengthy debate, chose the latter option and entered into a community-institutional cooperation with the Health Department.

Agnes Cobbs with friends and colleagues at her retirement. Dean Dan Shannon, former dean of outreach at UW-Milwaukee, far right. Dr. Belson Paulson and Reuben Harpole, center in back row.

The Task Force assisted the Health Department to secure a recently vacated elementary school as the site for the Health Center. This facility, renovated with federal community development funds, became a three story community health center and opened to the public in 1980. The new health center provided preventive care and outpatient curative medical services. The Harambee Health Task Force had not achieved all of the objectives on its ambitious agenda but this was a great step forward for Harambee residents.

Agnes Cobbs with "students" at her workshop on financial management, Martin Luther King Library. Her contributions to the community continue in retirement. 1992.

The Harambee Community Health Center was later renamed the Isaac Coggs Community Health Center, named after a well-known black Wisconsin state representative and Milwaukee County supervisor. The Harambee Task Force disbanded in 1979 and the community connection was assigned to the Isaac Coggs Health Center Advisory Committee, with members from the community, various local groups and the Milwaukee Urban League.

The Isaac Coggs Community Health Center is still in operation today. Harambee residents also have health services offered by a group of doctors, many of them involved in the Coggs Center in the early 1980s, through the Martin Luther King Health Center on King Drive.

Reuben Harpole, Belden Paulson and the members of the Harambee Health Committee and the Harambee Health Task Force should feel good about their great effort of the 1970s producing lasting effects to improve the health of Harambee residents over a 20-year period. All their objectives may not have been met, but there is a foundation that others can build on when the time is right.

NEIGHBORHOOD DEVELOPMENT IN THE 1990S

The Harambee community has seen a surge in support and community development activity since those early years in the 1970s. The Neighborhood and Family Initiative (NFI), started by the Milwaukee Foundation in 1990 with a $1 million grant from the Ford Foundation, has the mission of "building a strong, resourceful community whose residents define and control the future of the neighborhood." The NFI targets the issues of sufficient income, self-esteem, education and training, leadership development, physical and mental health, access to financial resources, real estate, decision-making, and a healthy environment.

The Center for Urban Community Development is still actively involved in the community. CUCD leadership has continued to work closely with the NFI through Kalyani Rai and Dan Folkman, who replaced Dr. Paulson as chair of the department in 1990.

The NFI operates with four task forces and committees. The Milwaukee Collaborative, formed by the Milwaukee Foundation with representatives of neighborhood interests and potential internal and external resources, provides governance for NFI and manages task force and committee activities.

NFI literature states that "There is a consensus among Collaborative members that Harambee residents for too long have lived with relative poverty and powerlessness in an affluent society which does not offer equal access to wealth and power. NFI's empowerment strategy builds upon and strengthens the capacities, skills and assets of Harambee families and the neighborhood. If NFI is successful, the active participation of Harambee residents and stakeholders will bring about neighborhood regeneration, growth and prosperity." The NFI can cite many accomplishments, including a revolving loan fund and a multitude of other projects supported through internal and external resources.

Reuben Harpole receiving one of many awards and citations for a life-time of contributions to the community. Orin Bradley, CEO and Chairman, Boston Store is honoring Harpole's contributions with the Kirkpatrick Award. December 1992.

Many individuals believe that the community leadership and social infrastructure created through the Harambee Revitalization Project of the 1970s attracted the Ford and Milwaukee Foundations to this neighborhood. If that is the case, the NFI is a continuing testament to the leadership of Dr. Belden Paulson, Reuben Harpole and Agnes Cobbs. They know the job is never done. The important thing is to have new carriers of the torch. In addition to the organizations that remain from the earlier era, the fact that a broader initiative with significant funding is continuing to work on comprehensive community development in the Harambee community is a tribute to the university-Harambee community leaders who invested so much of their time and talent a few decades ago.

DANGER SIGNALS
~ IN ~
CONSUMPTION

A poster for one of Extension's first public health programs listed the "danger signals" of tuberculosis, 1915.

(Courtesy, State Historical Society of Wisconsin)

RUN DOWN FEELING

LOSS OF WEIGHT

COUGH HANGING ON

FEVERISHNESS

BLOOD IN SPUTUM

INDIGESTION

LOSS OF APPETITE

DON'T RUN PAST THE DANGER SIGNALS

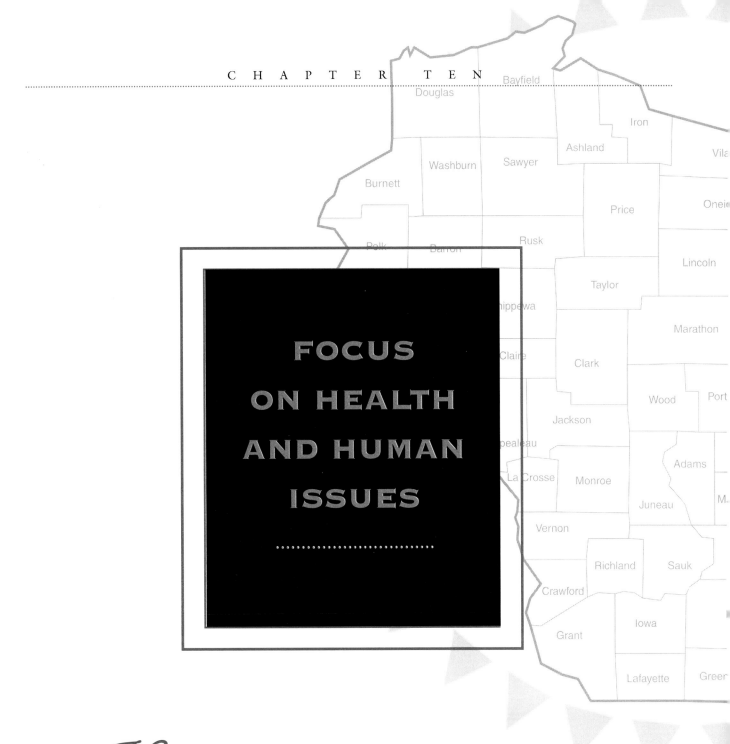

FOCUS
ON HEALTH
AND HUMAN
ISSUES

....

*N*eighbors helping neighbors. People organizing to help themselves and their mentally ill family members. Health and social service professionals and lay people of all ages forming alliances to advocate for prevention. These have been the professional and personal interests of Professor Roger T. Williams, Professor and Chairman of the Health and Human Issues Department at UW-Madison.

Roger Williams' strong interest in mutual support and self-help efforts led to his involvement in organizing the National Alliance for the Mentally Ill and the Wisconsin Alliance for the Mentally Ill. His interest in prevention and wellness led him to serve as a founding member of the Wisconsin Prevention Network. His interest in farm and rural issues led to the development of a Neighbor-to-Neighbor program to organize farm family support groups to cope with the farm crisis of the mid-1980s, and the Harvest of Hope Fund which disburses financial help to farm families in need.

ALLIANCE FOR THE MENTALLY ILL- NATIONAL AND STATE

Harriet Shetler and Beverly Young of the Dane County Alliance for the Mentally Ill, Inc. came to Roger Williams in 1979 to ask for help. They felt that families of mentally ill individuals were kept on the "outside," and that mental illness issues were dealt with only by professionals and largely swept under the carpet. The families wanted a voice.

This was the beginning of a strong partnership that responded to a deeply felt need. It created an organization to give a voice to families struggling with children or others with long-term, chronic mental illness. Roger Williams wrote a proposal to Title I for a $10,000 grant to convene a national conference. The hope was that a national organization would materialize out of the conference. Members of the Dane County Alliance brought their enthusiasm, commitment and hard work. The outcome was the conference, "Advocacy for Persons with Chronic Mental Illness: Building a Nationwide Network," co-sponsored by UW-Extension and the Dane County Alliance for the Mentally Ill, Inc. in September 1979.

The three days spent in Madison by 276 people from all over the nation generated great excitement. This was the first national conference for family members and friends of persons with chronic mental disabilities. Most of the people in attendance had worked ceaselessly at the local level to develop more humane and effective programs for family members. Many had initiated family support groups. This conference provided them with the prospect of forming a nationwide network of people and groups that could support each other and advocate with a unified voice on behalf of persons with long-term forms of mental illness.

The prospect became a reality on the morning of September 9, 1979, when the National Alliance for the Mentally Ill was formed. By that after-

Roger Williams. The rural and farm advocate. A professor who has made it his life's work to create and support self-help programs. (Photo: H. Shettler) 1986

noon, the Steering Committee, chosen from conference participants, had elected officers, selected committee chairpersons, and established priorities for moving ahead with incorporation as a national organization.

The Wisconsin Alliance for the Mentally Ill formed in 1980, following a similar conference format. Two important organizations were born. Williams could now pull back to advisor and educator roles.

Harriet Shetler of Madison is still involved in 1997. Having led

1986 Annual Convention marquee of the National Alliance for the Mentally Ill. (Photo: H. Shettler)

the organization in its infancy, she is now working on its newsletter. The President of the Dane County Alliance for the Mentally Ill in 1997 is Steve Pudlowski of the UW-Madison College of Engineering. President of the Wisconsin Alliance for the Mentally Ill is Dr. Robert Beilman, retired physician with the Dean Clinic. The Dane County chapter is 20 years old. Its current 450 members constitute the largest membership in its history.

Wisconsin has 35 local chapters of the Alliance, with 1,500 members. The National Alliance has about 1,000 chapters with 150,000 members. It has a budget of about $15 million. It is, indeed, a unified voice of advocacy on behalf of the mentally ill. Among its achievements are increased federal funding for basic research into mental illness and creating broad public awareness of the issues relating to mental illness.

The National Alliance is now focused on a Campaign to End Discrimination. In 1996 they built the campaign infrastructure. They've got a strong grassroots campaign organization, materials and public service announcements, and they are armed with studies and research documents to end discrimination against persons with mental illnesses.

The 1997 Campaign plan focuses on three areas: 1) Ensuring access to treatment and services for people with brain disorders (this is focused on insurance discrimination in benefit plans, HMOs and other managed care systems, and ending discrimination in public sector mental health systems); Getting opinion leaders to understand and act upon the key messages, namely that mental illnesses are brain disorders that can be effectively and affordably treated; and, 3) Building a coalition of business leaders, political and

DANE COUNTY ALLIANCE FOR THE MENTALLY ILL FOUNDING MEMBERS- 1977

Harriet Shetler, Co-chair

Beverly Young, Co-chair

Ben and Joan Lenski

Nancy Abraham

Betty Gulessarian

Bud and Jeanne Gourlie

Don and Kathy Kreul

Mike Kruel

Jeff Lenski

top-tier media representatives to broaden the support base of the National Alliance for the Mentally Ill.

Roger Williams, Harriet Shetler and Bev Young were right in their intuition back in 1979 that it was time to act. The outcome went far beyond their expectations.

WISCONSIN PREVENTION NETWORK

*R*oger Williams next applied the successful formula for creating a strong advocacy alliance for the mentally ill to prevention. A conference was organized in Rhinelander in October 1980 to bring together prevention professionals and interested lay persons. From this conference emerged the resolve to form a network of Wisconsin prevention workers. Within four short months, in January 1981, an organizing committee of 12 persons was selected to formulate the purpose, structure and by-laws of a statewide network and to move ahead with incorporation as a voluntary, non-profit organization: the Wisconsin Prevention Network (WPN).

WPN defines prevention as "a process which promotes health by empowering people with resources necessary to confront complex, stressful life conditions and by enabling individuals to lead personally satisfying, enriching lives." This definition suggests a two-pronged approach to prevention: a deliberate and constructive process to promote growth toward full human potential, and the counteraction of harmful circumstances such as stresses, pressures, economic distress and other hardships.

"WPN has always operated on a shoe-string. Prevention has never received the priority it deserves," remarks Williams.

It has, however, provided participants with technical assistance; a speakers bureau to educate individuals about prevention; a newsletter to keep people informed on emerging issues; an annual conference to build skills, share program ideas and organize for advocacy; and public policy updates alerting members to upcoming issues that can affect prevention. These alerts have

Nancy Abraham, at the podium, announcing awards. Left to right: Harriet Shetler, Beverly Young, Kathy Kreul and Dr. Donald Kreul (Founders of Dane County Alliance), David Lecount (Dane County Mental Health Coordinator). (Photo: H. Shetler)

been especially important during election and state budget years.

Roger Williams continued his support of the Network through its formative years. In addition to serving on the Board, he helped plan the first series of annual conferences and has co-chaired the Public Policy Committee since 1980. In recent years, the annual conferences have attracted 700-900 individuals, about half of them youth. Positive youth development has been a continuing major focus of the Network.

Of the many public policy initiatives undertaken by the WPN, the first big success came with the passage of *Right From The Start,* a legislative initiative that was signed into law by Governor Thompson in 1994. The focus of the legislation is to provide families with education and support so their children will be healthy, nurtured and valued as individuals. While it is aimed at reducing child abuse and neglect, the initiative is

Left to right: Nancy Abraham, founder of the Dane County Alliance for the Mentally Ill, Beverly Young and Harriet Shetler, founders of the National Association for the Mentally Ill.
(Photo: H. Shetler).

FIRST WPN BOARD OF DIRECTORS, 1981

Tom McDonald, Eau Claire

Kate Murphy, Madison

Laura La Vanway, Milwaukee

Ron Hering, Whitewater

Cindy Scott, Madison

Judy Schuknect, Friendship

Edith Valentine, Green Bay

Roger Williams, Cottage Grove

Bill Wilkinson, Milwaukee

Sharon Crooks, Milwaukee

Dan Kohn, Antigo

Karen Swan, Stevens Point

Ed Hammen, Appleton

Sharon Jaenke

intended to simultaneously improve the health and school readiness of children and have long term impacts on at-risk behaviors such as substance abuse, adolescent pregnancy, delinquency and teen suicide.

Right From The Start combines local, state and federal funds with private sources, such as United Way, hospitals, insurance companies and others, to encourage local action on behalf of children. Both as a concept and in its funding, this initiative may prove to be a model for future programs, and make a lasting social and economic contribution to the state and the nation. The importance of the Network is clearly evident in the list of organizations which endorsed the bill -- 115 different organizations were on record a year before the passage of the bill.

The Wisconsin Prevention Network has had an executive director since 1995. It continues its membership services of a quarterly newsletter, membership directory, at least two meetings in each of its seven regions per year, and public policy alerts. Activities for 1997 include the 15th annual Wisconsin Prevention Conference and staffing the state-funded Prevention Education and Training Task Force, Wisconsin Youth Coalition and *Right From The Start* Coalition. Its projects and activities continue to promote healthy families and communities throughout Wisconsin.

HARVEST OF HOPE

The Harvest of Hope is an initiative which combines Roger Williams' abiding interest in rural and family farm issues, his involvement with the faith community and his organizing skills. This is a fund which provides gifts to farm families who need financial assistance to purchase feed, fertilizer, fuel and other supplies for spring planting, and to meet emergency needs for food, home heating fuel, medical expenses, veterinary bills, machinery repair, electrical cut-offs, retraining or other immediate situations.

A Pick and Glean project for two farmers in the Cottage Grove area sensitized MCC members to the problems of Wisconsin farm families. (Photo: R. Williams)

The Harvest of Hope was created in January, 1986, in the midst of the Midwest farm crisis, to help people of faith take a stand in support of Wisconsin's family farmers. Roger Williams, Lois Koma and Emily Wixson -- all members of the Madison Christian Community (MCC) in Madison -- organized a Pick and Glean project to help two Cottage Grove farmers pick corn that couldn't be picked with mechanical pickers because the winter snows were too deep to get in the fields. The Pick and Glean involved 150 volunteers from the MCC and the Madison area, hand picking corn over the Martin Luther King, Jr. weekend in January, 1986. The event also sensitized MCC members to the problems of Wisconsin farmers. The Harvest of Hope evolved out of this effort and over $3,500 was collected from church members and sent to Wisconsin farm families in 1986.

Over its first eleven years, the fund has generated and dispersed over $400,000 to more than 750 Wisconsin farm families in difficult financial situations. The gifts average $520. The simple application is reviewed by a

Harvest of Hope Committee and a check is sent within two weeks. All administrative costs are covered by the host church, the Madison Christian Community, so every dollar contributed goes directly to farmers in need. People of all faiths qualify.

The fund represents a real partnership between the Madison Christian Community, the Wisconsin Conference of the United Church of Christ and the Wisconsin Conference of the

Roger Williams thanking Pick and Glean participants at a luncheon following the January, 1986 event. (Photo: R. Williams)

United Methodist Church. While many individuals and churches also contribute, there have been a few large contributors over the years, notably the Willie Nelson Farm Aid Program, the Kraft Dairy Trust Fund, the United Church Board for World Ministries and the South Central Synod of the Evangelical Lutheran Church of America.

Roger Williams has served as founder and chairman of the effort. The Harvest of Hope Committee consists of Dave Doerfert, Robert Forbess, Sara Hulsether, Howard Kanetzke, Tom Matthews, Randall Ney, Roger Williams and Margie Zamora.

The Harvest of Hope is elegant in its simplicity. It supports people's values, beliefs and hopes for the future. It is sharing and caring at its best. Much, much more of it is needed, but every small effort contributes to fostering hope among Wisconsin farm families.

Roger Williams thinks of himself as a catalyst, an educator and volunteer, a partner to many people, institutions and agencies. Whatever the issue, his strong belief in the importance of self-help and mutual support groups shapes his work and makes lasting contributions to the lives of people in need.

Extension's Nellie Kedzie Jones was behind the wheel of the tractor while serving as the state chair of the "Women's Land Army," which mobilized women for the war effort in World War I. Although she did not begin her career at Extension until 1918, Jones had been known in Wisconsin as an advocate of women's education and voting rights since the early 1900s.

(Courtesy, State Historical Society of Wisconsin)

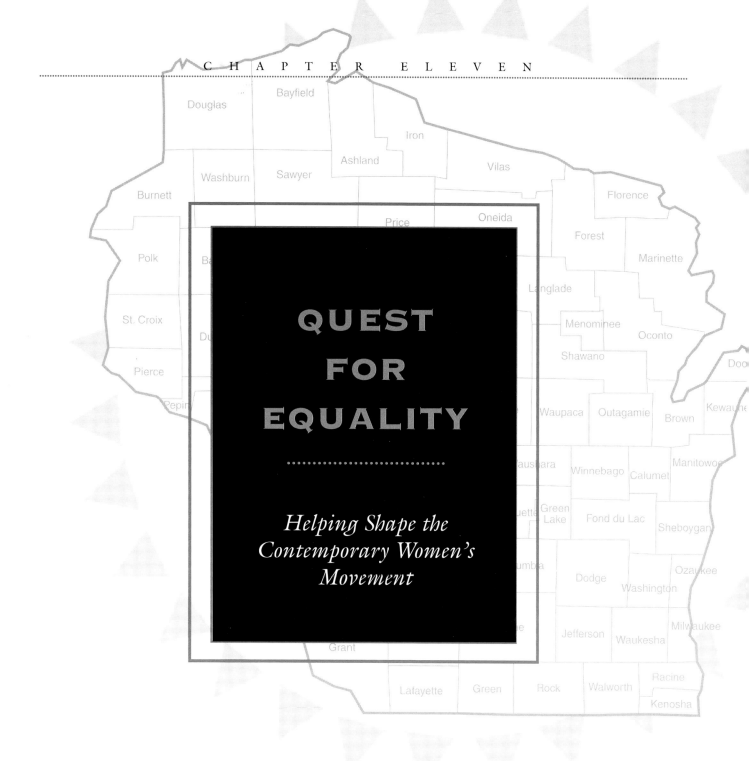

CHAPTER ELEVEN

QUEST FOR EQUALITY

· · · · · · · · · · · · · · · · ·

Helping Shape the Contemporary Women's Movement

"It was in the air," Marian L. Thompson said, when I asked why so many women's organizations devoted to the quest for equality started in the 1960s and '70s. It might have been in the air but there was more to it than that. A cadre of strong, intelligent women from all walks of life, with a passion for equality, had joined hands in Wisconsin and across the nation to build organizations that would set the policy agenda affecting women for decades to come.

In her correspondence-course guide entitled "Quest for Equality: A Look at the American Women's Movement," Constance Threinen explains that certain issues and events combined to create a new feminism in the early 1960s. The generation of women born after World War I had raised their children and were beginning to think of their own lives. They were thinking of completing interrupted college educations, of getting jobs, and of getting recognized for their contributions.

Betty Friedan wrote a book about all these changes; *"The Feminine Mystique"* suggested that women break out of their restricted lives as homemakers and take part in business and government. The Civil Rights Movement had also raised the consciousness of women. Finally, the focus of the United Nations on the "status of women" served as a catalyst for a series of recommendations and decisions which would focus attention on women's issues in the United States.

The focus of the United Nations staff was on the women of underdeveloped nations and their role in economic development. But, Eleanor Roosevelt, U.S. Delegate to the United Nations, seized the opportunity and recommended to President Kennedy to appoint a U.S. Commission on the Status of Women. President Kennedy appointed the U.S. Commission in December, 1961, asked Mrs. Roosevelt to chair it. Mrs. Roosevelt was greatly influential in shaping the Commission, but did not live to see its report, which provided the factual base

Kathryn Clarenbach, seated at right, and Governor Warren Knowles, with members of the Governor's Commission on the Status of Women, 1967. (UW Archives)

and working agenda for American women in their renewed quest for equality.

At about this time in Wisconsin, the spring of 1962, UW-Madison hired Kathryn Clarenbach to establish a program of Continuing Education for Women. This was the beginning of her leadership in the women's movement in Wisconsin and in the nation. Her office would later be joined with UW-Extension's Women's Education Resources Unit. The three women in this office, Kathryn Clarenbach, Constance Threinen and Marian Thompson, would combine their formidable strengths into more than two decades of leadership in the women's movement. They would inspire other women and organize to shape social legislation, such as marital property reform, which would affect the lives of Wisconsin women for all time.

Long-time colleagues Threinen and Thompson describe Kathryn Clarenbach as an imposing figure, with a unique ability to inspire and empower the women in her audiences. She stood tall, her vision was broad, and she was a born leader. She did not seek the limelight, but she had a formidable impact. As the following sections will highlight, Dr. Clarenbach was leading, organizing, chairing, building and shaping every important women's organization of her time. In her

Kathryn Clarenbach, fourth from right, President of the First Board of Interstate Association of the Commissions on the Status of Women, at the National Association of Commissions for Women Conference in Washington, D.C. at the Hilton Hotel, 1970. (UW Archives)

eulogy upon Kathryn Clarenbach's death in March of 1994, Judy Mann of *The Washington Post* called Kay Clarenbach "A Mother of Women's Rights." It was a fitting tribute to one who helped give birth to and shape a movement.

WISCONSIN GOVERNOR'S COMMISSION ON THE STATUS OF WOMEN

*T*he report of the U.S. Commission on the Status of Women, *American Women* (1963), recommended that women's organizations press their state governors to establish commissions on the status of women. In July 1963, Governor John W. Reynolds issued a press release indicating that he had asked Kathryn Clarenbach to call a statewide conference on the status of women, and making clear his intention to form such a commission.

The first Wisconsin Conference on the Status of Women, set to start on November 22, 1963, was cancelled upon news of President Kennedy's death. Connie Threinen remembers arguing with her colleagues that the conference should proceed because, "President Kennedy would have wanted us to get on with this important work." She was out-voted.

The first Wisconsin Conference on the Status of Women reconvened in

RECIPE FOR FRUSTRATION

From *"New Directions For Women"* used in publicity for Wisconsin International Women's Year Meeting for 1,000+ women, June 1977. The national conference was held in Houston, Nov. 18-22, 1977.

1 cup crushed ego

1 teaspoon job discrimination

1/4 teaspoon chauvinism

1 well-beaten path to the washing machine

1/2 teaspoon grated nerves

1 pinch from a man on the street

1 dash from the dentist to the babysitter

Mix all ingredients, one on top of the other, and stir violently. Cook until you feel a slow burn and add one last straw.

Serves 53% of the population.

January 1964, at the Wisconsin Center in Madison. Kathryn Clarenbach chaired the conference. Anthropologist Ethel Alpenfels keynoted the conference, which 350 people attended. The proceedings were widely distributed, with an inventory of the issues affecting women as the significant output of the conference.

KATHRYN CLARENBACH

A Mother Of Women's Rights
Professor of Political Science
October 7, 1920 - March 4, 1994

UNIVERSITY WORK ON BEHALF OF WOMEN:

◆ Convener and Secretary of the University of Wisconsin Faculty Women's Association (1970-71)

◆ Chair of the Governor's Commission on the Status of Women (1964-69, 1971-79)

◆ First President of the National Association of Commissions for Women (1970-72)

◆ A founder and first Chair of the Board of the National Association for Women (1966-70)

◆ Member of NOW Advisory Council (1971-1978)

◆ President of NOW Legal Defense and Education Fund (1982-1983)

◆ Chair of the National Organizing Conference of the National Women's Political Caucus (1977)

◆ Member and Executive Director of the U.S. Commission for Observance of International Women's Year (1975-76)

◆ Deputy Coordinator of the Houston National Women's Conference (1977)

◆ Board member of the National Women's Conference Committee (1978-92)

◆ Officer of the Wisconsin Women's Network (1979-82, 1985-1986) and the Wisconsin Women's Council (1983-89)

◆ Founder and officer of the National Forum for Women (1983-1986)

◆ Vice-President of the Southwest Wisconsin Coalition of Labor Union Women (1982-83)

◆ First lay chair of the Board of Trustees (1968-72) and member of the President's Advisory Council (1977-80) of Alverno College.

◆ Wife of Henry G. Clarenbach, mother of three, Director of University Education for Women from 1962 to 1967, and UW-Extension Specialist, Continuing Education for Women from 1967 to 1972. Professor of Political Science, Department of Governmental Affairs until her retirement in 1988.

In May 1964, Governor Reynolds appointed the Governor's Commission on the Status of Women. Wisconsin was the 25th state to set up a commission. Kathryn Clarenbach was named chair and served in this role until 1969, and again from 1970 to 1979. Under her leadership, the Commission worked with women's organizations on statutory reforms to reduce discrimination and provide greater opportunities for women. Clarenbach also represented Wisconsin at meetings of the National Association of Commissions on Women, and served as the first president of that association from 1970 to 1972.

The Commission received its support from UW-Madison and UW-Extension for its formative years. In 1973, nine years after its formation, the Legislature voted a budget of $20,000 per year for the commission, over strong opposition to any budget. The Commission could now hire its first staff, Norma Briggs, as executive secretary.

Kathryn Clarenbach, Bella Abzug and Gene Boyer. Three Contemporary Feminist Leaders. (From: C. Threinen, Quest for Equality: A Look at the American Women's Movement. High School Course Guide, 1990).

Illustrative of the Commission's contributions was its focus on sex stereotyping in the schools. At the Commission's urging, State Superintendent of Public Instruction Barbara Thompson established the Task Force on Sex Role Stereotyping in the School in 1976. Connie Threinen of UW-Extension was appointed chair. This task force, after months of study, put forth a plan of action and produced evaluative and training materials for school administrators and teachers. It also recommended a model policy for this purpose. The preferred approach was one of self-assessment by teachers and administrators, using the materials developed by the task force.

First Women's Equality Day in Beaver Dam, August 26, 1970. Businesswoman and organizer Gene Boyer calls it a one-woman parade... No one joined. (Gene Boyer)

The Governor's Commission on the Status of Women officially closed down on June 30, 1979. Along with the termination announcement, Governor Lee Dreyfus announced the establishment of the Governor's Advisor for Women's Initiatives as a member of the Governor's Executive Staff. The GCSW thus became a special chapter in the quest for equality.

Wisconsin's commission is considered to have been one of the most active and influential commissions in the nation. It took on a multitude of issues and problems confronting women -- equal rights, employment, health benefits, day care, divorce, family planning, legal and economic status of homemakers, women offenders and many more issues of importance to women. It made its mark through good research, published material, testimony at public hearings for or against proposed legislation, public speaking and interviews by members. Marian Thompson cited the marital property reform legislation to be the last hurrah of the Commission's 15 years of work and "a fitting memorial to an organization which has symbolized public recognition and concern for women's issues."

"It is naive to assume that because we are right, we'll win. We must generate the mail and lobbying activity to influence the Legislature. We must also educate the general public. Finally, we must defeat those who are now in office who stand in the way."

(Paraphrased from National Women's Political Caucus newsletter *Call to Action on the ERA.*)

In 1983, with the leadership of Governor Tony Earl, the Wisconsin Legislature established the Wisconsin Women's Council. The mission of this 15-member council is to eliminate the barriers to women's equality, and to advance the economic, social, and educational status of all Wisconsin women. The funding of the Wisconsin Women's Council is not commensurate with the importance of its mission.

NATIONAL ORGANIZATION FOR WOMEN (NOW)

Members of the State Commissions on the Status of Women were annually invited to Washington, D.C., to share information and brainstorm approaches to overcome discrimination against women. The Women's Bureau at the U.S. Department of Labor provided support for

League of Women Voters' function in the early 1960s. Connie Threinen, Representative Dave O'Malley, Senator Carl Thompson, Marian Thompson and JoAnne Gillings.

the U.S. Commission, as well as for these meetings. While the meetings served a very useful purpose in terms of information exchange, they were also frustrating in that state commission members were not free to take strong positions on issues and to lobby for them. The prohibition against lobbying by public agencies limited their freedom to act.

During the third National Conference of State Commissions in Washington, D.C., a few women met in Betty Friedan's hotel room. They discussed the frustration of being unable to lobby for policies which would address the very issues they were discussing at these conferences. They felt a strong need for a new organization which could complement the activities of the state commissions. The National Organization for Women was born that night in the hotel room. Among those present were Kathryn Clarenbach and Gene Boyer, from Beaver Dam.

On the final day of the conference, the National Organization for

NaNNaNNaN

Women (NOW) was formally organized. Among the original 27 members, 11 were from Wisconsin. At the organizing conference of NOW, four Wisconsin Women were elected to the national board: Catherine Conroy, Sister Joel Read, Sister Austin Doherty, and Kathryn Clarenbach, who was elected as national chair of the board. Betty Friedan was elected as NOW's first president.

NOW played a key role in organizing the women's movement for action on a broad-based agenda. It organized support for the Equal Rights Amendment (ERA), lobbied for its passage in both houses of Congress in 1972, and worked for the approval of the ERA in 35 states, just three short of the two-thirds needed for ratification. This drive lost momentum and died in 1982, but its consciousness-raising effects formed the foundation for many other legislative initiatives in the quest for equality.

NOW membership was 300 in 1967, the first year of this new organization. NOW counted 250,000 men and women among its members by 1980, a number that remained constant from then on.

Judy Goldsmith of Wisconsin giving the President's speech at the annual meeting of the National Organization for Women, October, 1982. (Gene Boyer)

NATIONAL WOMEN'S POLITICAL CAUCUS

The National Organization for Women was a leader in the creation of the National Women's Political Caucus in 1971. More than 300 women from all over the country met in Washington, D.C., on July 10-11, 1971, to form the first National Women's Political Caucus. Four Wisconsin women attended this meeting — Betty Smith, past chair of the Governor's Commission on the Status of Women; Mary Louise Symon, Dane County Board member; Marjorie (Midge) Miller, Wisconsin State Assembly Representative from Madison; and Kathryn Clarenbach, chair of the Governor's Commission on the Status of Women. Clarenbach chaired this historic meeting. Midge Miller was elected to the National Caucus Board.

MARIAN L. THOMPSON

A native of Syracuse, New York, and educated at Mt. Holyoke College and the University of Wisconsin-Madison, Marian Thompson had a 27 year career with UW-Extension as a specialist in Women's Education. Working closely with Kathryn Clarenbach and Constance Threinen, she focused her talents on helping women of all socio-economic groups increase their self esteem by acquiring new skills and competencies.

She served for 20 years on the Legislative Committee of the League of Women Voters of Wisconsin. She chaired the Wisconsin Women's Network for three years and edited its newsletter. She was a charter member of ARC Services, an agency helping women offenders and their children.

Her unique contributions to the Wisconsin Women's Movement have been as a researcher and as the editor of the *Wisconsin Women* newsletter. This widely-shared informational quarterly chronicled the issues and actors, the successes and failures of an exciting time for the Women's Movement between 1970 and 1984.

Marian remains an activist and a civic contributor since her retirement in 1989.

Wisconsin delegation that went to the National Women's Conference in 1977. (Gene Boyer)

The Caucus was made up of a remarkably broad cross-section of women -- by color, income, political persuasion, occupation and organization. Labor leaders, civil rights leaders, members of Church Women United, League of Women Voters, elected officials representing all levels of government, housewives, and the National Council of Negro Women were among the many present at this meeting. Their goals were elegantly simple: to encourage women candidates to run for office and to promote the election of candidates who will support the issues of deep concern to women. State-level political caucuses were the local manifestation of this initiative. The Wisconsin Women's Political Caucus held its first state convention at UW-Milwaukee in January 1973.

The national and state caucuses were diligent in urging women to run for office and in supporting the election of women to policy-making positions at all levels of government. But their impact went far beyond the early vision. They urged caucus members to participate in the selection of delegates to the national conventions of their own political parties. They got pledges from both major parties to work toward 50% representation of women. They also publicized the voting records of office holders and the known views of candidates on women's issues.

It was a complete and multi-faceted political strategy. It was so successful that a new generation of women take for granted the opportunity to hold public office, by election or appointment, a quarter-century later.

WISCONSIN WOMEN'S NETWORK

The National Women's Conference, held in Houston, Texas in 1977 in celebration of the International Women's Year, adopted a National Plan of Action, which was developed after a series of state meetings held throughout the country, involving more than 130,000 participants. The Wisconsin International Women's Year Conference was chaired by Connie Threinen. This conference,

Catherine Conroy, Kathryn Clarenbach, Betty Friedan, Gene Boyer after a speech by Friedan. October, 1981. (Gene Boyer)

involving more than 1,000 men and women, featured photo exhibits, workshops, and prominent keynote speakers. It also elected delegates to the Houston conference and provided input to the National Plan of Action.

The publication, *Wisconsin Women and the National Plan of Action*, identified the need "to create a network of Wisconsin women and men to facilitate coordination, provide a communications system and strengthen the advocacy voice for women's issues." The idea was endorsed by the Houston conference.

In 1979, there were many organizations which supported policy development around issues of importance to women. But communication and coordination were missing. The major impetus for building the Wisconsin Women's Network came when Governor Dreyfus decided to disband the Governor's Commission on the Status of Women.

The Wisconsin Women's

GENE BOYER

Gene Boyer is a trail blazer and an organizer. Among her legendary skills related by friends is the ability to draw up the by-laws of a new women's organization before the brain-storming ends! She's had a lot of practice. She helped form the Beaver Dam Mayor's Commission on Women, the Wisconsin Governor's Commission on the Status of Women, the Wisconsin Women's Network, Wisconsin Business Women's Coalition, and Women Business Owners of Wisconsin.

On the national front, she was in Washington at the Status of Women Commissions Conference in 1966, helped found NOW and served as its national treasurer and financial development officer, as well as a board member of the NOW Legal Defense and Education Fund, which she chaired in 1993. She also helped activate women's networks in Washington, Missouri, Colorado, Florida and New York.

Boyer also helped organize the National Association of Commissions on Women, National Women's Political Caucus, National Association of Women Business Owners, and the National Women's Conference Center, which she has chaired since 1981.

Boyer is currently a professional public speaker and owns Gene Boyer & Associates, Inc. which offers a full range of consulting services to small business owners. Needless to say, she remains an activist on issues concerning women.

JUDY GOLDSMITH

Judy Goldsmith, a Wisconsin native, was raised by her divorced mother who worked in factories for 25 years. She and her four siblings knew poverty as children. A scholarship allowed her to attend UW-Stevens Point for her B.A. in English, and she earned a master's degree at the State University of New York at Buffalo. She taught college English for 15 years before becoming a national officer of NOW in 1978.

Goldsmith served NOW both as national executive vice president (1978-82) and as president (1982-85), having risen through the ranks beginning with local and state involvement in Wisconsin.

As NOW president, she led the organization through some of the most visible and effective activity in its history, including NOW's role in the selection of Geraldine Ferraro as the first woman to run as a vice-presidential candidate on a major party ticket; and NOW's focus on civil rights, including Goldsmith's arrest in 1984 at the South African Embassy in protest of apartheid policies and her co-chairing the 1983 March on Washington with Coretta Scott King.

Her NOW administration also concentrated on economic issues affecting women, including pay equity, affirmative action, pensions, reproductive health issues, social security, and child care.

Goldsmith served as Special Consultant to the Chancellor for Equity and Affirmative Action at UW-Stevens Point (1991-93) and currently serves as Campus Dean at the University of Wisconsin Center-Fond du Lac.

Network was formed in the fall of 1979. "The power of women as an effective constituency must begin to be felt," stated Gene Boyer of Beaver Dam, an established leader in the Women's Movement. Another founder, Kathryn Clarenbach added, "..there has long been a need for independent powerful voices speaking out loudly and clearly on issues of concern to women without fear of reprisal. The Wisconsin Women's Network will meet that need."

The founding organizations included the Wisconsin Women's Political Caucus, Coalition of Labor Union Women, Wisconsin NOW, Wisconsin Civil Liberties Union, the League of Women Voters, the Center for Public Representation, the American Association of University Women, and many others. Serving on the first Network board were prominent Wisconsin women, including Liesl Blockstein, Gene Boyer, Kathryn Clarenbach, Catherine Conroy, Joan Dramm, Eunice Edgar, Eleanor Fitch, Nelia Olivencia, Vel Phillips, Chris Roerden, and Louise Trubek. Helen Casper of Madison was employed as the primary staff person. Gene Boyer chaired the Network.

The Network, which continues today, is not a membership organization. It is a vehicle to provide information, communication links and advocacy services to existing organizations to strengthen their abilities to function. It was the final step by the leadership of the Wisconsin Women's Movement to strengthen the individual organizations they had helped build.

LIST OF MAJOR POLICY INITIATIVES AND SUCCESSES OF THE CONTEMPORARY WOMEN'S MOVEMENT

*M*aternity leave, affirmative action, marital property reform, family planning, legalized abortion, nondiscrimination in employment, poverty programs, day care, integrate help-wanted ads, sexism in schools, Title IX of the 1972 Amendments to the Higher Education Act prohibiting discrimination in higher education institutions receiving federal funds, opportunities in athletics, domestic abuse, health benefits for women, teenage pregnancy, women offenders, credit, feminization of welfare, flexible hours, rape laws, pornography, displaced homemakers, inheritance, comparable worth.

CONSTANCE F. THREINEN

Connie Threinen, a native of Massachusetts, attended Mt. Holyoke College before transferring to UW-Madison upon the advice of her father, a UW-Madison alumnus. She graduated with honors in labor economics and also met her husband, Bill, there. The move was, truly, Wisconsin's gain.

Threinen coordinated UW-Extension's and UW-Madison's outreach classes for women for 27 years, retiring in 1989. In a 1968 interview, she described her work as "helping women lead more interesting and useful lives." She, indeed, enriched the lives of many thousands of men and women through her coverage of many subjects, ranging from international economic issues to the visual arts, securing experts to teach the subjects in every corner of the state. She was the "outreach teacher" in the formidable trio of Clarenbach-Thompson-Threinen for high school students which she wrote, titled "Quest for Equality: A Look at the American Women's Movement."

The Wisconsin Women's Network, which she helped found, selected her as the 1994 Stateswoman of the Year. The award highlighted her decades-long commitment to equal rights for women and girls. She organized and chaired the 1977 State Conference on International Women's Year in Madison, was a founder of the National Women's Political Caucus of Wisconsin, served as a delegate to the National Women's Conference in 1977, chaired the Task Force on Sex Role Stereotyping for the Wisconsin Department of Public Instruction in 1975-76, and was a leader and member of countless other women's and girl's issues task forces and boards.

But, Threinen's labor of love has always been the League of Women Voters. A member since 1948, she has served on the boards of the Madison, Middleton and Wisconsin Leagues and has served as president of the Middleton League in 1959 and 1962-64, as well as chairing the Legislative Committee of the Wisconsin League since 1956. Since retirement, she has focused her energy and talents on land use and economic issues. But, she is still the women's advocate and the nurturer of the organizations she and her colleagues helped found. Her quest for equality continues to benefit new generations.

Young people attending an Extension Youth Program session on the grounds of the College of Agriculture, Madison, 1928.

(Courtesy, State Historical Society of Wisconsin)

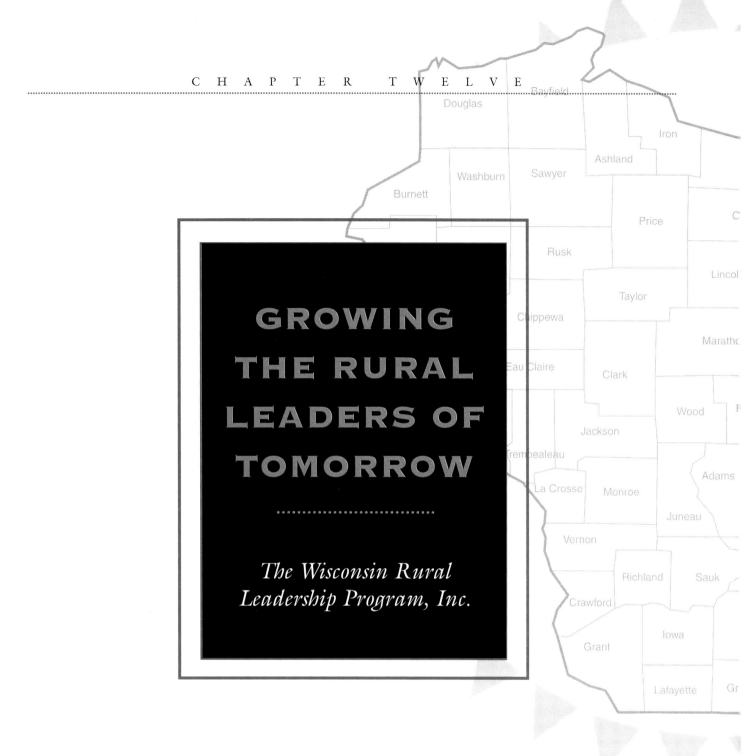

CHAPTER TWELVE

GROWING THE RURAL LEADERS OF TOMORROW

•••••••••••••••••••••••••••

*The Wisconsin Rural
Leadership Program, Inc.*

𝒯ake a group of young men and women between the ages of 25 and 50 who have already demonstrated leadership. Expose them to people, ideas and issues they would not otherwise encounter. Arrange for them to travel to other parts of the United States and the world to broaden their perspective. Give them the analytical tools to make sound decisions. Sharpen their communication skills and connect them to a growing network of leaders. You would then have the Wisconsin Rural Leadership Program (WRLP).

(135)

Rural Wisconsin is part of a regional, national and international political and economic system. A broad understanding of the forces at work in Wisconsin, the nation and the world is necessary for effective leadership. Community development research clearly identifies the existence of effective local leadership as the single most important determinant of vibrant communities. The Wisconsin Rural Leadership Program was developed to produce effective rural leaders for the future.

Presidents of the Board of Directors of WRLP, Inc. Left to right: Thomas Lindahl, Steve Zillmer, Diane Pavelski, Russ O'Harrow. (Alan Herrman missing)

Now in its 14th year, this strong public-private partnership has graduated about 180 leaders as of 1997. Five of them have served in the Wisconsin Legislature and most of the others are involved in community, county and state level leadership cutting across all sectors of Wisconsin.

At the heart of this unique organization is the concept of shared leadership. The corporation is governed by a board of directors composed of government agency leaders, University of Wisconsin administrators and private sector representatives. Governors Tony Earl, Lee Sherman Dreyfus and Tommy Thompson have served on the board. The board makes policy, approves the curriculum, selects the groups and raises funds for the endowment. The board also contracts with the University of Wisconsin-Extension to develop and administer the educational program. There is strong participation from the faculties of UW-Madison, UW-River Falls, UW-Stevens Point, UW-Platteville, and other campuses of the UW System in seminar leadership and teaching.

The WRLP Alumni Association keeps WRLP graduates in touch with each other and supports their continuing learning activities. The alumni constitute a formidable reservoir of leadership talent

PRESIDENTS OF WRLP BOARD OF DIRECTORS

1983-88 **Russell O'Harrow** Oconto Falls, President of the UW Board of Regents, Agricultural Leader

1988-91 **Alan Herrman** Green Bay, Manager of Business Development, Wisconsin Public Service

1991-93 **Steve Zillmer** Watertown, General Manager, River Valley Cooperative

1993-95 **Diane Pavelski** Platteville, Dean, College of Advancement, Chippewa Valley Technical College

1995-97 **Thomas Lindahl** Platteville, Dean, College of Business, Industry, Life Science and Agriculture, UW-Platteville

BELOW: Executive Directors with Mary Maier, manager and the "heart" of the program since its beginning. Left to right: Dick Barrows, Gerry Campbell, Mary Maier, Lowell Klessig, Ayse Somersan. Missing: Bob Pricer, Bob Rieck.

for both rural and urban communities of Wisconsin.

The birth and history of WRLP is a classic case of vision and collaboration. It is also a great example of building on the experience of others and improving on it.

Wisconsin didn't invent this wheel! Early work on the project began in 1980 when CALS Dean Leo Walsh responded to an invitation from the W.K.Kellogg Foundation to send representatives to an informational meeting in Spokane, Washington. Those attending included Stephen Smith (UW-Madison), Roger Swanson (UW-River Falls), and Laura Beane (agricultural leader from Jefferson County). They heard favorable reports on Kellogg-sponsored leadership programs that had been going on in Michigan, Washington, Montana, California and Pennsylvania.

On January 9, 1981, the Agricultural and Natural Resource Consortium of the University of Wisconsin System approved preparation of a draft proposal to initiate a rural leadership development program in Wisconsin. The meeting was chaired by Al Beaver, UW System administrator and Consortium executive secretary (now Acting Chancellor of UW-Extension). Gale VandeBerg, director of Cooperative Extension, was asked to take the lead in contacting faculty to further develop the idea and the proposal. UW-Extension was asked to administer and coordinate the project. Richard Barrows, professor of Agricultural Economics and extension specialist at UW-Madison, volunteered to contact state leaders and develop the proposal.

ABOVE: Mark Cook and Mark Boyke of Group III at the National Seminar in Washington D.C. 1989.

WRLP EXECUTIVE DIRECTORS

Group I: **Richard Barrows**
UW-Madison/Extension

Group II: **Robert Rieck**
UW-Extension

Group III: **Ayse Somersan**
UW-Madison/Extension

Group IV: **Robert Pricer**
UW-Madison/Extension

Group V: **Gerald Campbell**
UW-Stevens Point/Extension

Group VI: **Lowell Klessig**
UW-Stevens Point/Extension

Group VII: **Alan Anderson**
UW-Extension

TOP: Board members: Patricia Goodrich, Carl Ohm, Barbara George. LEFT: Judy Wiff and Jeanetta Robinson during the Urban Issues Seminar for Group VI in Milwaukee. 1995.

During 1982 and 1983, key leaders met to determine support for the proposal. Consensus was reached. In May 1983, a proposal was submitted to W.K. Kellogg Foundation by the director of Cooperative Extension with the approval of a provisional board of directors.

In September 1983, the board of directors was officially organized. They approved a curriculum proposal from the university and a fund-raising strategy which officially launched the program. Dick Barrows, serving as the executive director of the program, initiated recruitment for Group I. Faculty and the board began planning the curriculum. Group I was selected in April 1984 and attended their first seminar in July 1984. Group I participants completed the series of eleven seminars in March 1986.

The leadership on the board and the participants reflect the diversity of Wisconsin's rural communities. WRLP is not an agricultural leadership

Left to right: Alan Tank, Norm Monsen, Bang Van Le of the Vietnam Embassy, Karen Dahl, Joel Kroenke, Dale Bowe of Group VII during their National Seminar in Washington, D.C. 1997.

development program. Board members and participants come from all sectors and professions -- tourism, agriculture, business, government, health and the nonprofit sector, and they are not all rural and white. Urban Wisconsinites participate in the program, as do Native Americans, blacks and hispanics.

The program continues to have strong leadership on the board, through significant membership from WRLP alumni and other leaders. Through state support from a line-item budget allocation, continuing strong support from the University of Wisconsin institutions, in terms of both budget and faculty involvement, and a long term endowment of over $500,000 raised by board members, WRLP is in stable financial condition.

WRLP does not consider itself a training ground for future legislators, mayors or governors. It develops leaders with broad perspectives to serve their communities. It is, however, a foregone conclusion that some future "household names" in politics will proudly wear WRLP graduation pins on their lapels.

BELOW: Al Rankin of Group V during the International Seminar in Mexico. 1993.

CURRICULUM FOR GROUP VII--1996-98

State Government Seminar, Madison
Topic: Welfare Reform

Leadership Seminar, Treehaven, Tomahawk

Urban Issues, Milwaukee

Education Seminar, Janesville

National Seminar, Washington D.C.
Topic: Foreign Policy

Health Issues Seminar, LaCrosse

Regional Seminar, State of Oregon
Topic: Natural Resources Issues

Community Issues Seminar, Richland Center

International Seminar, Thailand, Vietnam, Hong Kong

Family Issues Seminar, Oshkosh

Natural Resources Seminar, Kemp Station, Minoqua

THE FOUNDERS — PROVISIONAL BOARD OF WRLP

LaVerne Ausman, Secretary,

Laura Beane, Dairy Farmer, Fort Atkinson

Albert Beaver, Senior Academic Planner, UW System Administration

Tom Brogan, Executive Vice Chairman, Northern Hardwood and Pine Manufacturers Association, Green Bay

David Coggins, Farm Credit Bank, St. Paul

John Cottingham, Deputy Secretary, Wisconsin Department of Agriculture, Trade and Consumer Protection

Paul DeMaine, Native American Liaison, Executive Office of the Governor

Charles DeNure, Dean, College of Agriculture, UW-Platteville

Anthony Earl, Governor, State of Wisconsin

Rockne Flowers, Chairman, Nelson Industries, Inc.

John Gasser, NFO, Sauk City

Millard Gunlach, Dairy Farmer, Montford

Don Haldeman, President, Wisconsin Farm Bureau Federation

Thor Hansen, Weyerhaeuser Company, Schofield

Keith Hawkes, Wisconsin Public Service Corporation, Green Bay

Celia Lausted, Dairy Farmer, Colfax

Russell Leitch, CEO, Inland Foundation, Inc., Milwaukee

Mike Lomperski, Associate Director, Wisconsin Bankers Association

Pat Luby, Vice President, Oscar Mayer Foods Corporation

Tom Lyon, General Manager, Midwest Breeders Cooperative

Dick McNall, McNall Equipment, Inc., Janesville

Mary Lynn Meyer, Wisconsin Association of Manufacturers and Commerce

Lee Mulder, President, Wisconsin Farmers Union, Chippewa Falls

Nyla Musser, Extension Home Economist, Jackson County

Leo Nickash, United Paper Workers International Union

Rod Nilsestuen, Executive Secretary, Wisconsin Federation of Cooperatives

Tom O'Connell, Extension Agricultural Agent, Dane County

Russ O'Harrow, UW Regent and Dairy Farmer, Oconto Falls

Leonard Peck, Dairy Farmer, Chippewa Falls

Stan Peterson, Insurance and Real Estate, La Crosse

Walter Renk, Seed Corn/Beef Farmer, Sun Prairie

James Richardson, Vice President, Aid Association for Lutherans, Appleton

Bob Rieck, Dean, Cooperative Extension, UW-Extension

Gary Rohde, Dean, College of Agriculture, UW-River Falls

Steve Smith, Dean, School of Natural Resources, UW-Madison

Carl Theiler, Executive Secretary, Wisconsin/Michigan Timber Producers Association

Dan Trainer, Dean, College of Natural Resources, UW-Stevens Point

Dean Treptow, President, Brown Deer Bank

Lester Wallace, Master, Wisconsin State Grange

Leo Walsh, Dean, College of Agriculture and Life Sciences, UW-Madison

Bob Walton, President, American Breeders Service, DeForest

Lori Ward, Associate Editor, *Hoard's Dairyman*

Russ Weisensel, Executive Director, Wisconsin Agribusiness Council

Ralph Yohe, *Wisconsin Agriculturist*

Marilyn Zirbel, President, State Board of Vocational Technical and Adult Education, Dairy Farmer, Bristol

TOP: Founding team: Bob Rieck, Russ O'Harrow, Leo Walsh. ABOVE: Jim Leverich, Jane Barnett, Sandra Cihlar of Group IV at their National Seminar in Washington, D.C., 1991.

Group I *Standing from left: Pete VanWychen, Paul Taylor, Douglas Porter, Lee Jensen, Michael Kopchik, Robert MacSwain, Heidi Kohlwey Schultz, Donald Genrich, Thomos Albrecht, Thomas Beane, Diane Zilisch, Thomas Syverud, Deborah Reinhart, Raymond Diederich, Barbara George, Pete Knigge, Alvin Ott, Frederick Wyttenbach, Kim Zuhlke, James Stowell, Michael Whitty, Richard Barrows. Seated, from left: Dorothy Reeder, Jane Grabarski, Lois Van Someren, Nancy Danielson, Helen Torphy, Sheila Harsdorf, Sherin Bowen.*

Group II *Back Row - Robert Klussendorf, Charles O'Harrow, Grayson Zuhlke, Steve Emmerich, Dick Pernsteiner, Jane Fellenz, Russell Moyer, Gregory Zwold, Edward Liegel, Roger Luckow. Second Row - Thomas Breunig, Stanley Szymanski, Susan Krull Schultz, Nodji VanWychen, Laurie Jarvis, Judy Klusman, Fred Capelle, Colleen Nilsestuen, Fran Renn. First Row - James Winter, Delayne Green, Ole Meland, Anita Genrich, Stanley Kaczmarek, Faye Thunder, Karl Klessig, Shirley Bargander, Dave Doniels. Not pictured - Francette Hamilton, Michoel Malcheski and Bernard Ziegeweid.*

Group III *Back Row - Linda Hodorff, Gary Steele, David Natzke, Douglas Gray, Mark Boyke, Laurie Golden, Mark Cook, Sheryl Albers, Connie Scharlau. Middle Row - Chris Schwenck, Phyllis Fritsch, Sara LaBarge, Rebecca Gutzman, Jane Nee, Mark Misch, Ken Day, Paul Proctor, Jack Mlsna, Steve Pinnow, Lorraine Beyersdorf, Carol Cox, Richard Karls, Debra Diederich, Marvin Kiesow. First Row - Judy Klahn, Daphne Hultermun, Jean Schomisch, Nancy Caldwell, Joan Kruse, Maxine Luchterhand. Not pictured - Jeff Saatkamp.*

Group IV *Top Row - Harvey Menn, Paul Dietmann, Jack Hippen, Leo Johnson, Bruce Holsclaw. Third Row - Phillip Brenizer, Roger Neumann, Luther Olsen, Janice Hirth, Jerry Knoll, Jim Raymond, Dan Renzoni. Second Row - Mary Jo Borneman, Kathy Overman, Jim Leverich, Connie Julka, Judy Poler, Charles Radloff, Jim Massey, Glenn Smith, Scott Zimmerman. First Row - Gershia Coggs, Bernard Kuenne, Gary Princl, Sandi Cihlar, Donna Justin, Jane Barnett, Linda Peterson, Edward Weber, Lindsey Driver.*

Group V *Top Row - Gary Kirking, Gregory Hines, Dale Stange, Randy Ullmer, Dan Deneen, Paul Hermanson, Jim Curns. Third Row - Tim Klusman, Randy Treml, Mark Finger, Arnold Fritsch, Mark Gunn, Tom Winker. Second Row - Dennis Quinn, Jeff Bradley, Alva Rankin, Sue Baumer, Bruce Kraus, Theresa Olsen, Scot Wall. First Row - JoDee Sattler, Anna Maenner, George Danner, Bryce Larson, Brad Brunner, Beverly Hoege, Joyce Roth.*

Group VI *Row 3 - Jim Holte, George Johnson, Jim Schoenike, Jim Heinen, Jeff Schinzing, Patrick Sorge, Michael Kroenke, Bryon Renk, Nile Beck, Bob Cullen, Barbara Lee. Row 2 - Lowell Klessig, Chuck Dallas, Tom Reichert, Brian Kindschi, Connie Loden, Mark Peacock, Margaret Wepner, John Koss, Ellen Hooker, Eileen Nickels, Mary Maier. Row 1 - Tami Karls, Judy Wiff, Jim Nelsen, Jean Henderson, Michael Moore, Sandra Dlask, Greg Erickson, Carrie Pierquet, JoAnn Moedke, Steve Stark. Not pictured - Brent Bergstrom and Douglas Moericke.*

Group VII *TopRow: Alan Tank, Peter Kling, Robert Nigh, Paul Solberg, Brian Spencer, Joel Kroenke, Greg Schopen, Norm Monsen, Dale Bowe, Sam Miller. Middle Row: Charles Tubbs, Mary Maier, Karen Dahl, Victoria Harter, Gloria Hafemeister, Cathy Reuter, Al Anderson, Craig O'Leary, David Jelinski, Sandy Heidel, Diane Kaufmann, Mary Housner. Bottom Row: Mary Millard, Jean Hundertmark, Bonnie Peterson, Mark Mayer, Sandy Houle, Lori Bocher, Viluck Kue, Donna Barnes-Haesemeyer, Jerry Sinkula, Catherine Techtmann, Marie Pitre. Not pictured - Karna Hanna.*

WISCONSIN RURAL LEADERSHIP PROGRAM
Groups I-VII
Home counties of participants.

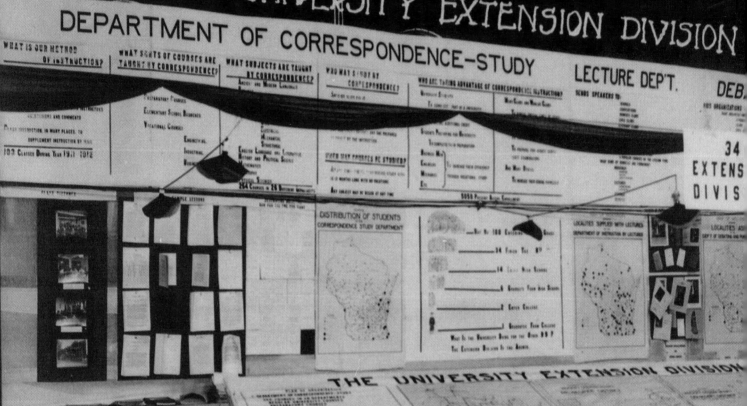

An exhibit of Extension Division programs at Madison in 1912 featured correspondence studies as the means to make the boundaries of the university the boundaries of the state.

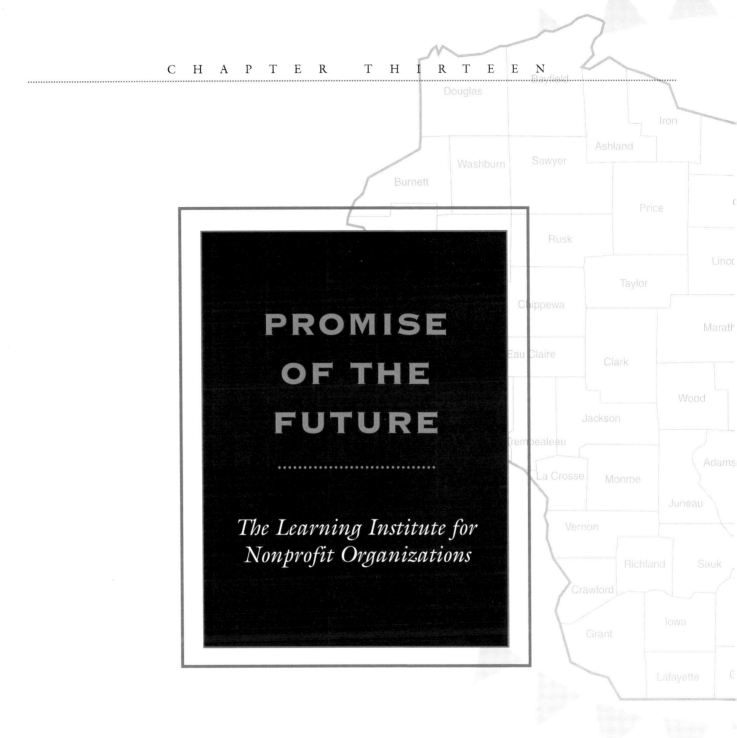

PROMISE
OF THE
FUTURE

••••••••••••••••••••••

The Learning Institute for
Nonprofit Organizations

*T*imes change. Needs change. The post-World War II era was a time of building

organizations and associations in the state, and University of Wisconsin faculty took part

on all fronts. Now it is time to develop the educational and technical support for non-

profit organizations like those highlighted in this book and the many other organizations

which make vital contributions to the quality of life and the economy in communities

across the nation.

The nonprofit sector is the fastest growing part of the nation's economy. It is estimated to contribute over $535 billion a year and employ 8.6 million people. Nonprofit organizations often take the lead in human service delivery, cultural affairs, education, health, research, the arts, and community development.

The Learning Institute for Nonprofit Organizations of Madison, Wisconsin is a unique organization. It is a collaboration among a for-profit corporation, Murphy Communications, Inc., a non-profit organization, the Society for Nonprofit Organizations, and a university, University of Wisconsin-Extension. The partnership brings together the distance-education, continuing-professional-development and non-profit-sector-expertise of the diverse partners and greatly expands the existing base of professional development opportunities for nonprofit leaders and their organizations. It is designed to strengthen nonprofit organizations and the communities they serve.

The Learning Institute is the brainchild of Professor Terry Gibson of UW-Madison/Extension and Katie Burnham, founder and executive director of the Society for Nonprofit Organizations. They were strongly supported and encouraged in their early developmental efforts by former Chancellor of UW-Extension Donald Hanna and David Sanks, Vice President and General Manager of Murphy Communications, Inc. Also lending strong support to the idea was the Board of Directors of the Society for Nonprofit Organizations.

Professor Terry Gibson, UW-Extension (left) and Katie Burnham, Executive Director were the creative partners who developed the proposal for the Learning Institute which got W.K. Kellogg Foundation funding of $1.5 million to provide educational support to the nonprofits sector. 1997.

Press Conference in the Governor's meeting room, announcing the Kellogg Foundation grant. Left to right: Andy Lewis, Community Development Director for the Learning Institute, Katie Burnham, Executive Director of the Learning Institute, Lt. Gov. Scott McCallum, David Sanks, General Manager WISC TV and representing Murphy Communications, Inc., Donald Hanna, former Chancellor of UW-Extension. 1996.

The Learning Institute became a reality in 1996 with a $1.5 million grant to the Society for Nonprofit Organizations by the W.K. Kellogg Foundation, "to promote and strengthen nonprofit sector leadership and management through a new collaborative approach to distance education. "The collaborative approach and the idea of testing this partnership as a demonstration model was a primary reason for the significant financial support by the W.K. Kellogg Foundation.

The comprehensive curriculum of the Learning Institute incorporates the core principles of governance, leadership and management delivered through interactive, live satellite programs, on-site teaching and follow-up, audio, video and print materials, computer access through the Internet and expert assistance through phone and e-mail.

ORGANIZATIONS REPRESENTED ON THE NATIONAL ADVISORY BOARD OF THE LEARNING INSTITUTE

National Civic League

Ripon College

Center for Living Democracy

Energize, Inc.

Institute for Transformation of Learning

Points of Light Foundation

National Community Education Assn.

American Family Insurance

AARP-Wisconsin

Center for Nonprofit Management

Oshkosh Foundation

Public Allies Milwaukee

National Center for

Charitable Statistics

Katie Burnham received the 1997 Wisconsin Idea Award from UW-Extension. She represents the new generation of leaders who continue to seek a strong relationship with their public University in new and creative ways to serve Wisconsin and the nation.

THE LEARNING INSTITUTE PARTNERS

Murphy Communications, Inc. - a family-held corporation with a 40-year history of community involvement and participation in projects, business development and civic initiatives. Its focus in distance learning is on the development and distribution of educational products intended by use by adults, children, families and the community.

The Society for Nonprofit Organizations- a 501(c)(3) nonprofit national membership organization that serves as a clearinghouse of information and facilitates wide-ranging education, training, and support services. It seeks to draw together all elements of the nonprofit world, encourages open communication and sharing, and fosters a sense of community in the sector.

The University of Wisconsin-Extension - through its programming divisions of Cooperative Extension, Extension Communications, Continuing Education Extension, and collaborative relationships with 26 UW campuses, 72 Wisconsin counties, and countless local, state, and federal agencies and groups, provides a spectrum of lifelong learning opportunities for all Wisconsin residents.

UW-Extension Awards Ceremony, May 15, 1997. Katie Burnham accepts the Wisconsin Idea Award on behalf of the Learning Institute. Left to right: Peter Coolsen, Program Director of Learning Institute, Katie Burnham, Interim Chancellor Albert Beaver, Dr. Mary Brintnall-Peterson, Community Education Director of LI and professor with UWEX, Andy Lewis, Community Development Director of LI.

SOURCES

I. PUBLISHED HISTORICAL MATERIAL CONSULTED

Fifty Years of Cooperative Extension in Wisconsin, 1912-1962, University of Wisconsin Extension Service, College of Agriculture, Circular 602, Madison, January, 1962, and Circular 602-Supplement, January, 1963.

PROGRESS in Wisconsin through the Extension Service, College of Agriculture, School of Home Economics, Special Circular 104, University of Wisconsin, Madison, April, 1965.

Grace W. White, Cooperative Extension in Wisconsin: 1962-1982, Kendall/Hunt Publishing Company, Iowa, 1985.

John J. Jenkins, A Centennial History, A History of the College of Agricultural and Life Sciences at the University of Wisconsin-Madison, CALS, University of Wisconsin-Madison, 1991.

Jack Clark, "The Wisconsin Idea: The University's Service to the State", State of Wisconsin BLUE BOOK, 1995-96, Wisconsin Legislature, 1995, pp. 101-179.

II. MATERIAL (PUBLISHED AND UNPUBLISHED) USED IN SPECIFIC CASE STUDIES.

Chapter One: The Arts

School of the Arts at Rhinelander, Our 25th Anniversary, 1964-1988.

The Wisconsin Youth Symphony Orchestras, 25th Anniversary 1966-91

"PROGRESS in Wisconsin through the Extension Service", University of Wisconsin, Madison, Special Circular 104, April 1965.

John W. Jenkins, A Centennial History, A History of the College of Agricultural and Life Sciences at the University of Wisconsin-Madison, UW-Madison, 1991.

Wisconsin Foundation for the Arts, Inc., Governor's Awards in Support of the Arts, November 1992.

Fannie Taylor, "Arts Support Goes Public in Wisconsin", WASAL Transaction, Vol. 68, 1980.

Robert Gard, et. al., The Arts in the Small Community, A National Plan, The Office of Community Arts Development, University Extension, U.W.-Madison, in association with the National Endowment for the Arts, Washington, D.C., 1969.

Grace W. White, Cooperative Extension in Wisconsin: 1962-1982, Kendall/Hunt Publishers, Iowa, 1985.

Support Gratefully Acknowledged: Harv Thompson, Cedric Vig, Jerry Apps, Dick Wolf, Dave Peterson, Pat Blankenburg, Jeff Bartell, Dean Amhaus, Ted Shannon, Elayne Clipper-Nelson, Bob Graves, Fannie Taylor, George Tzougros.

Chapter 2: Wisconsin Farm Progress Days

Personal files of Henry Ahlgren and Al Francour.

Historical files of Wisconsin Farm Progress Days, Inc. Office.

Support gratefully acknowledged: Henry Ahlgren, Donald Peterson, Al Francour, Art Peterson.

Chapter 3: Cooperatives

T. Torgerson, Building Markets and People Cooperatively: The Lake to Lake Story.

Reports of the Governor's Dairy Marketing Committee, 1960.

Fifty Years of Cooperative Extension in Wisconsin, 1912-1962. UW Extension Service, College of Agriculture, Madison, Circular 602, January 1962.

"PROGRESS in Wisconsin through the Extension Service." Special Circular 104, University of Wisconsin, Madison, April 1965.

T. Graf, "Fifty Years of Dairy Marketing — Key Developments," paper presented at the 50th Annual Midwest Milk Marketing conference.

Grace W. White, Cooperative Extension in Wisconsin: 1962-1982, Kendall/Hunt Publishers, Iowa, 1985.

Support Gratefully Acknowledged: Truman Graf, Frank Groves, Joan Behr of Foremost Farms, Peter Giacomini, Rod Nilsestuen, Richard Vilstrup

Chapter 4: Forage Councils

Records of Emeritus Professor Dwayne Rohweder; UW-Madison/Extension Agronomist Dan Undersander.

Chapter 5: Forestry

Fifty Years of Cooperative Extension in Wisconsin, 1912-1962, University of Wisconsin, Madison, 1962.

Fred Trenk - Annual Reports, Department of Forestry files, UW-Madison.

R. Giese, et. al., A Historical Account of Forestry at the University of Wisconsin, Unpublished report, 1983.

Thomas Rausch, WWOA, 1979-89: A Look At Our First Ten Years.

Support gratefully acknowledged: Ron Giese, Ted Peterson, Gordon Cunningham, Chris Hauge, Thomas Rausch.

Chapter 6: Lakes Partnership

Managing Wisconsin's Inland Lakes, The Role of the University of Wisconsin Extension, Progress Report, 1976.

Lake Tides, A Newsletter for People Interested in Wisconsin Lakes.

The WALD EAGLE, Newsletter of the Wisconsin Association of Lake Districts.

The Lake Connection, Newsletter of Wisconsin Association of Lakes, Inc.

The Wisconsin Lakes Partnership, Fact Sheet, UW-Extension Lake Management Program, College of Natural Resources, UW-Stevens Point.

Support Gratefully Acknowledged: Lowell Klessig, Robert Korth

Chapter 7: Tourism

Personal files of Donald Schink.

Historical files of the Wisconsin Tourism Federation.

Support gratefully acknowledged: Donald Schink, Herman Smith, Gene Radloff, Sue Sadowske, Thomas Coenen.

Chapter 8: Kickapoo Reserve

The Kickapoo Valley Reforestation Fund, At Work in the Kickapoo Valley, 1995 Annual Report, School of Natural Resources, College of Agricultural and Life Sciences, UW-Madison.

Eric Wuennenberg, "Rejection, Redemption and Renewal", in Silent Sports, August 1994, pp. 29-34.

Douglas Bradley, "Lighting a Flame in the Kickapoo Valley", in Wisconsin Ideas, UW-System, April, 1994.

Personal files and newspaper clippings of Alan Anderson.

Support gratefully acknowledged: Alan Anderson, Marcy West

Chapter 9: Urban Neighborhoods

RESOURCE MATERIALS:

Belden Paulson and Daniel Folkman, A Reporting and Planning Model for Urban Community Development: A Case Study in Community-University Participation, UW-Extension, December, 1976.

E.D. Clarke and Steve Paulson, The Harambee Health Experiment, Center for Urban Community Development, UW-Extension, 1983.

Neighborhood and Family Initiative fact sheet and strategic plan.

Harambee Ombudsman Project, Inc. Fact Sheet

Individual Support Gratefully Acknowledged: Dr. Belden Paulson, Reuben Harpole, Agnes Cobbs.

Chapter 10: Health and Human Issues

NAMI Campaign to End Discrimination letter

Proceedings of ADVOCACY FOR PERSONS WITH CHRONIC MENTAL ILLNESS: BUILDING A NATIONWIDE NETWORK Conference, 1979.

Wisconsin Prevention Network brochure, newsletters and concept paper on prevention.

Harvest of Hope brochure and ten year report.

Support Gratefully Acknowledged: Roger Williams, Harriet Shetler.

Chapter 11: Quest for Equality

Marian Thompson, Wisconsin Women Newsletter, 1970-1984.

Connie Threinen, Quest for Equality: A Look at the American Women's Movement, A High School Course, UW-Extension, Independent Learning.

Gerda Lerner, Oral History Project. Tapes at State Historical Society.

Materials from "Bridges That Carry Us Over," Conference on Midwestern Leaders of the Modern Women's Movement. Women's Studies Research Center, Women's Studies Program, UW-Madison, November, 1992.

"On Wisconsin Women", Chronology of Recent Highlights of Wisconsin's Women's Movement (1962-1977), June, 1977. Prepared for Wisconsin International Women's Year Meeting.

Support Gratefully Acknowledged: Connie Threinen, Marian Thompson.

Chapter 12: Rural Leadership

Historical files of the Wisconsin Rural Leadership Program, Inc. Office.

Support gratefully acknowledged: Alan Anderson, Mary Maier.

Chapter 13: Learning Institute

Learning Institute for Nonprofit Organizations, Grant Proposal to W.K. Kellogg Foundation, 1996.

Brochures of The Learning Institute for Nonprofit Organizations.

Support Gratefully Acknowledged: Terry Gibson, Katie Burnham.

III. PERSONAL INTERVIEWS AND INDIVIDUAL FILES OF FACULTY AND STAFF.

See Acknowledgements p. 4

INDEX